Prepared to Survive

Guide For Survival

Margot Dillard, Author
Copyright 2020
Updated 2022
United States of America
Independently Published
ISBN: 9798672083162

Sections

About the Author

Margot Dillard has put her interests to paper, as her varied non-fiction works will attest. Many rely on her knowledge and the life experiences that she shares.

She has pursued a hobby of wine appreciation and created "how to" wine books and humorous looks at life from the bottom of a wine glass to playing in the dirt. Her wine books include; Life by the Glassful, What's all the Wine-ing About, Wine, and Sweet Words.

The Essential Oil books were notes and tips Margot had created for herself and decided to share; Let's Learn About Essential Oils, The Basic Essential Oil Kit, and her most popular book, Essential Oil Recipes.

Divorce...I Said I Do, But I Don't is not based on her personal experience but on seeing the need for a humorous take that she shared with friends going through a tough time.

Her newest book, Planting for Honeybees and Pollinators, as well as her garden tips and peaceful garden quotes book, Life in the Garden, is based on playing in the dirt on her 11-acre property.

An Affliction Named Golf is a group of facts, history, and quotes she has gathered as both a golf widow and a player. Her more serious pursuits, one just completed, Prepared to Survive, is about planning for a significant life event such as COVID-19 or something far more severe.

Introduction

I wrote this book to provide sound, practical information for people that want to be prepared for whatever life throws their way. With the recent COVID-19 pandemic, I thought this book might have a broader scope and purpose for extended in-home Isolation that wasn't initially considered. I was in the process of editing the initial format of this book before a Pandemic hit worldwide.

 Are you prepared for a killer storm, major power outage, a viral pandemic, political instability, or an act of terrorism that would impact you or your family for more than several days? Regardless of the reason or severity of the event, a little pre-planning can go a long way to ensuring your family's care and well-being. COVID-19 showed how events impact our fragile life systems and food sources.

The answer is usually a resounding "NO" when asked if you are prepared!   Maybe you and your family could 'rough it' for several days. Still, unless you have a plan and are ready for an emergency, you are likely unable to deal with issues such as storms or pandemics lasting weeks to a much longer and larger life events.

Many people pooh-pooh the idea of preparing emergency plans and believe they can get what they need at the last minute. Finding food, fuel, and gear at the last moment is difficult for anyone living in a highly-populated area when a massive winter snowstorm or hurricane is expected. For those that experienced the 2020 Coronavirus (COVID-19), you experienced shortages of items never considered a "hoarded item."

Ask yourself if the Boy Scout needs all the skill training and badges they earn. Those boys might never use their training, but their motto, "Be Prepared," is about being ready to respond if needed. Planning for an emergency and never having to enact the plan is a much better choice than being reactive without proper preparation.

Update December 2022-

COVID-19 vaccines were made available; today, there is still controversy around getting vaccines. Test kits are readily available for at-home testing. There are still many restrictions and mask-wearing required in certain areas. Life is as normal as possible but has never returned to pre-COVID-19 status.

Shortages continue to pop up in different areas, highlighting how fragile our country's infrastructure remains. Another crisis, on top of this one, could have created even more significant impacts on lives.

Our lesson is that a seemingly minor worldwide event has effects lasting more than two years, so always be prepared.

Planning

Is planning for a potential emergency just being paranoid or being prepared? Some people are natural planners; they need to be organized and ready for whatever life throws their way. There is nothing paranoid about being prepared.

Other people insist that dangerous situations or emergencies will never happen to them. Is this crazy or insane? To a prepper, it sounds insane. Think of the major hurricanes, floods, and other deadly storms in your lifetime. Would the people in those storms want to be prepared?

Life isn't all blue sky and sunny days, but it is also not doomsday. There has to be a middle ground of preparedness without paranoia. Years ago, our relatives were more self-sufficient and less dependent on companies and stores to fulfill everyday needs. People had gardens, root cellars, and supplies to avoid long store trips. They were prepared for more than just a day or two.

The time to repair the roof is when the sun is shining. President John F. Kennedy

Today, we live day to day or week to week with our supplies, mainly due to the ease with which we can quickly meet our needs. We quite simply are an instant impact society that's getting all of our supplies sent to us via Next Day Delivery! Is this a crazy way to live?

Being paranoid is not a natural mindset or way of life and is often underscored with unreasonable fear. Fear, when moderated, is healthy as it keeps us from danger and prepares us for a crisis. Response from fear is either a fight, flight or freeze response. When we face a severe storm, a pandemic, or another emergency, freezing is not acceptable, flight may be necessary (with sufficient supplies), and better yet, being ready and prepared to fight is best.

Unless you lived as a hermit or under a rock in 2020, you have no doubt realized how much easier your life might have been with preparation and planning. In America, we saw what was beginning around the globe, but few people reacted fast enough to avoid food and product shortages. Under government-mandated shutdowns due to the Coronavirus (COVID-19) virus and stay-at-home isolation orders, goods online and in stores quickly disappeared.

In addition to the storms brought about by nature, the media creates another level of fear and danger that intensifies the potential for additional fear and paranoia. The media creates a sense of impending doom and that we are victims. We do not need to be paranoid and fear-filled. Nor do we need to be victims.

If only you had planned for this!
What is your plan in a disaster?

Different emergencies and situations require different types of planning or degrees of preparation for various emergencies. Preparing for a weather-related emergency would have given you some necessary supplies for a week or so of support with the COVID-19 virus. Families ready for other troubles would have been better suited to this newly imposed viral emergency, as stores quickly ran out of essential supplies.

Make sure you know the types of disasters you are likely to incur in your locality and create various plans to mitigate the risks. At a minimum, you should have a storm protocol and an Isolation plan. The first step is to define if this is a "Stay in Place," a "Weather Event," or a "Grab a Go Bag" event. The event type requires different approaches, yet some of the Go Bag items will be useful when confined to your home, specifically a general emergency kit that will work for most situations and fit the needs of the people in your plan.

Ensuring that your preparation plan provides vital elements for success is essential. You can help yourself and others by sharing your ideas and getting validation from their feedback. Additionally, creating plans, assembling kits, and periodically checking your supplies and training sessions will help identify customization requirements for your situation.

The safety and care of your family are too important to rely on an ad-hoc approach, so let's begin to look at some basics.

Planning without action is futile; action without planning is fatal.

General Planning or Emergency Specific

Few people would have anticipated the United States closing down for a dangerous virus. Each state also issued Executive Orders detailing what businesses could open, how many people could gather, and much more. Besides, vast shortages of certain products were encountered and continued for months. At the time of publishing, the country is still experiencing prolonged impacts.

Our country's infrastructure could not easily handle such a widespread emergency and the heavy use or hoarding of critical supplies. At first, it seemed like it was just a matter of quickly restocking and getting in new shipments to offset what hoarders and those looking to sell goods at an inflated price had scooped up.

Limits, if the items could be found, were placed on these everyday items and more:

- o   rubbing alcohol,
- o   hand sanitizer,
- o   disinfecting cleaning products, Lysol, Clorox, etc
- o   face masks,
- o   sterile gloves,
- o   bottled water,
- o   paper products – toilet tissue and paper towels
- o   basic foods – flour, sugar, yeast, salt, bread mixes
- o   foodstuffs, such as macaroni and cheese, prepared/boxed meals, peanut butter, dairy products
- o   Meats –limited to 2 items of beef, chicken, and pork

After several months of shortages, items did appear to be restocking, except for critical supplies needed for the medical profession treating COVID-19. Alcohol, sanitizers, masks, and gloves were still like gambling, either luck was with you, or you continued to find empty shelves, most likely open space.

As the weeks wore on, more people working in the industries that the government deemed "Essential Services" became infected, and many work and production facilities could not implement social distancing.   The production at meat processing plants was shut down due to the high level of infection, adding to concerns about how much meat you could buy. Further, grocery prices jumped for the first time in more than a decade due to limited supply and growing demand.

It's not about being fearful but being ready to react appropriately.

This type of pandemic event was unforeseen. It would bring unemployment to significant heights, limit our supplies, and, where possible, have people working from home. We can prepare for future events like this by avoiding shortages for our families. "Stay at Home" orders and self-isolation did not mean we needed to incur food shortages or a lack of sanitizing products if we had only been ready.

Typically, we would plan for a stay-at-home event based on weather conditions and have our weather kit ready. It would likely include some of the items that were critical during our recent pandemic; Milk, Bread, Toilet Paper, Paper Towels, etc.

Depending on the area of the country you live in and the weather conditions for that region, you may want to specialize in a weather kit.   Inform yourself on how to prepare for many weather hazards. It is also reasonable to have a "What to do" plan for human-made disasters such as wildfires, hazardous material incidents, environmental conditions, and terrorist acts.

The following pages will give you tips and information that can be used to ensure you have a basic isolation kit or a Go Bag that contains items for general survival or specific incidents, particularly weather for your area. Additionally, the planning should consider the location for a disaster. Are you in your home or the car, or do you need to leave the safety of your home?

Preparing for different situations can necessitate other planning and materials. Packing and storing contents for a disaster in your home versus surviving in the wild can result in very different items being stored. Wilderness sustainment requires camping-style equipment, while holding up in your home to wait out a storm or disaster doesn't require the ability to pack and carry your provisions.

There is a minimum of three types of plans; home, weather, and wilderness. We will be looking at the stay safe at home planning, with several primary grab-and-go kits that can be used in any scenario. A weather kit is essential for surviving the outdoors if you need to go into the backwoods for any reason. Also, we need to plan for disasters resulting from manufactured violence.

When you're dying of thirst, it's too late to think about digging a well.

Six months after the COVID-19 Pandemic started, major grocery stores were still not fully stocked on paper products, meats, and basics such as flour and sugar.   Grocery pickup and delivery services added thousands of jobs in stores, as people were reluctant to shop. Regardless of ordering online or in the store, getting all the items you wanted was a game of luck.

If not required in each state, Masks were highly recommended, and the term "social distancing" by remaining six feet apart was applied everywhere. In my area of the country, signs were posted on all businesses, and aisles in stores were marked to make them one way to help people stay apart and keep the traffic flow going.

We will look at preparing for "Staying in your Home" first, then address the added issues of needing to stay put for "Weather" and, finally, "Wilderness" survival.

"Good preparation is better than hope for a miracle."

Staying in your Home

Think you can outlast a significant storm or disaster at home? Unless you plan and have prepared supplies, you aren't ready! Waiting until a disaster is about to strike is not the time to try and throw a few things together. Having your home-based survival items ready and waiting is as necessary as being prepared to survive outdoors.

The "home plan" items might vary slightly from items packed in a "grab bag" kit, and the quantities that can be stored, particularly food and water, aren't limited to what you can carry. Having your sustainment checklist for emergency planning is simply a smart start. While the intent of riding out a situation in your home is your primary plan, thoughtful planning would assume that you may need to leave your home. Be prepared for both conditions.

Keep your HEAD concept applies to all situations:

H – *Have* your supplies *handy* and let people know if you are staying put or leaving.

E –*Essentials* are a priority, so make sure your supplies are viable…food has not expired, water is fresh, and kits are stocked.

A-*Assets* needed to survive a minimum of a week without power, heat, and foods that can be prepared with what you have.

D- *Deal* with the situation, *don't panic* when an emergency occurs. Keep calm, and ensure that you protect your supplies.

Don't wait for a severe event to test your plan. Think ahead, practice with your family, and have a home and wilderness kit ready.

Surviving at Home

Until the impact of COVID-19, the primary concern of survival in a home was most likely a weather event that could have affected your need to survive without heat/cooling, water, and power. Having a roof over your head is great, but you must keep yourself comfortable and cook food.

Surviving at home is the most straightforward event to plan. Depending on your family's situation, you would base your plan upon the number of people in your home, your pets, and allergies or diet preferences.

With a pandemic, the needs of your home isolation are different, as your power, phone, and water supply are likely to remain unchanged. However, as we all quickly learned with COVID-19, the ability to get all the food items and products we needed was difficult. Imposed limits on meats and foods of 1 or 2 packages don't work well for a large family.

Within days of the cases hitting the USA, supplies of sanitizers, cleaners, rubbing alcohol, nitrile gloves, and masks were off the shelves, and nothing remained online. Products of this nature were also designated for medical and first responders.

After just a few weeks of the infection rate and death counts starting to rise, the federal and state governments issued isolation notices. Schools were closed, restaurant dining was stopped, all non-essential businesses were closed, workers were told to work from home, and hours were shortened for companies that remained open. Additionally, any open place was required to implement "social distancing" and limit people allowed into stores.

By the time the everyday person reacted, there were already critical shortages, and seven weeks into the pandemic, deficiencies still existed and were expected to last much longer. Being prepared would have helped most of us from being impacted.

While last-minute preparation for storm events typically creates a rush on food and paper products, it would usually just be a short time before the store restocked shelves. The widespread infection across the country impacted our principal food producers and their employees. Supplies would not be keeping up with demand. Stores placed limits on the number of products, particularly meat, customers could purchase.

In April 2020, Tyson Foods. A significant meat processor took out a full-page ad in the New York Times to address the potential meat shortage, saying that the **"food supply chain is breaking."**

Tyson's noted that "livestock and poultry processing plants have been shuttered by coronavirus outbreaks among workers." It was estimated U.S. pork processing capacity is down, with three of the largest pork processing plants in the U.S. closed. Processing was down, and prices started rising.

Shortages of products such as meat directly resulted from COVID-19, as it was impossible to keep workers separated by six feet during the viral pandemic. Because processing is operating at about 60% of standard capacity, daily limits of purchases were made. An Executive order by the government was made to keep the food chain going.

The White House issued a Fact Sheet, "Closure of a single large beef processing plant can result in the loss of over 10 million servings of beef in a single day. Similarly, the closure of a single plant can eliminate more than 80 percent of the supply of a particular meat product—like ground beef—to an entire grocery store chain." Sadly, the food supply chain was already impacted, and long-term shortages would continue.

All is not lost; even late preparation is better than sticking your head in the sand and thinking this is ending or will never happen again. Let's get started!

By failing to prepare,

you are preparing to fail.

Benjamin Franklin

Food Storage at Home

Most people can't imagine being stuck at home for weeks on end. The COVI 19 virus forced Stay at Home orders across the country. If you or someone in your family tested positive for COVID-19, your family was quarantined for fourteen days. Having food on hand and adequately stored was necessary, as we couldn't run out and get whatever we wanted when we wanted it.

 Properly stored and packaged, foods can last ten years or more. Understanding how long foods last and how best to keep them is the basis of prepping food. But most importantly, have a cache of foods you and your family will eat. Sauerkraut, macaroni, and vinegar won't do anyone any good unless you can provide enough calories to support your family. They also will need to eat the foods you have.

The advantage that sustainment in the home has is the number of supplies you can have stored versus your need to carry what you eat. Sealed containers, cans, and jugs can hold a wider variety of foods and liquids to balance primary food groups better. Proteins, grains, fruits, and vegetables are all readily available for storage.

Understanding how to store food and what foods have the most extended shelf life is an early step in preparing for a disaster. Again, we must point out that waiting for weather or national service alert is **not** the time to prepare!

Without freezing, storing bread is not possible for extended times, but flour, yeast, eggs, or cornmeal lets you make various grain products. Having the basics ready is essential if you want these items. These items will be gone immediately at the beginning of a disaster or panic-buying episode.

During COVID-19, everyone learned how quickly loaves of bread disappeared from shelves, along with yeast, flour, and cornmeal. The disappearing Milk, Bread, and Toilet Paper game frequently happens during bad storms but only lasts a few days. Finding these items during COVID-19 was like going on a scavenger hunt and losing! COVID-19 may have been the first time a food shortage impacted your life, but make sure it's the last time this has happened to you.

Knowing how to make substitutions and what you can use instead of missing items is also essential. For the first time in years and years, we have seen a failure in the production and delivery of our essential foods, staples we have only run out of for a few days or a week, not months or longer. You can't store eggs, which were also in short supply, but you can have powered eggs for an emergency.

Preparation is a proceeding or readiness for a future event as a goal and an acceptable outcome. Wikipedia definition

According to the United States Department of Agriculture (USDA), foods that can be safely stored at room temperature are called "shelf-stable." These non-perishable products include jerky, country hams, canned and bottled foods, rice, pasta, flour, sugar, spices, oils, and foods processed in aseptic. These packages are usually marked as not requiring refrigeration until after opening.

Perishables are treated by heat or dried to destroy foodborne microorganisms that can cause illness or spoil food, such as botulism, to be considered shelf-stable. Commercial food packaging is subject to regulation, and when purchasing or storing items, watch out for dented or bulging cans. These are signs of spoilage.

Home-canned items are not subject to the care and handling of commercial packaging but the diligence of the preparer. When opening canning jars, ensure the seal is intact; visual and auditory signs should be noted.

Foods that are not stable for survival storage would be labeled as "Keep Refrigerated." When preparing for an event that could mean massive, long-term power loss, remove any food requiring refrigeration from potential storage items. Storing foods that require freezing to extend shelf life will work in a limited scope. Once a disaster hits and the power is off, any bets for storage life are skewed against you. For example, butter will last up to ten years in a freezer, but butter will only last for months when not frozen.

Having a storage area and system for food rotation is your starting point. Knowing the substitutions you can make is also good to know. Store canned foods and other shelf-stable products in a cool, dry place; below 85°F is best. Many examples of shelving systems can be built or purchased for arranging canned goods. Marking the items with the date they are added to storage is a good idea for tracking.

Not only should your food supply be checked for signs of compromised quality, but they should always be exchanged and kept as fresh as possible. Finding out during a disaster that your food is beyond usable is a mistake that can cause hunger or illness.

Don't confuse the "sell by" or "use by date" marked on containers with how long foods can be stored! The USDA states that Dating is for quality, not safety.

Cool, dry, and dark are watchwords for the preparer. Making your food last as long as possible and safely will mean the difference between wasting money and having a robust food supply. Food should not be left in boxes and bags but stored in sealed jars or containers.

The FDA and the United States Department of Agriculture (USDA) do not mandate that foods are date labeled! However, the FDA issues the Food Code model so that there is a standard for states to use if they choose.

Shelf Stable Products

The Use By date and the Best By date aren't the final date that people can eat food. Foods on the grocery shelf will last much longer than the date that food manufacturers put on products. Most of the items that are marked on your grocery shelve will last much longer. Part of the dating process is to have you quickly use and replace products rapidly, making you spend more, and the producer earns more. Yet, some products have enhanced taste by the stamped date, but being past that date doesn't necessarily mean the foods have become inedible.

You want to ensure that you are storing items properly to keep foods at their best, but you also should know that available shelf lives are suggested for each type of food. The length of time for storage and rotation is controlled by you and your system for labeling and storing. The kind of preparation of the food can also make a difference, as noted in the chart.

**What does "shelf-stable" mean?
A person can safely store foods at room temperature or "on the shelf," which is called shelf-stable. FSIS/USDA**

Storage Guidance

The conditions and containers used for foods can impact food quality and viability. In optimal storage areas, food can safely be used for extended periods. The following guidance is generally accepted, but in all cases, the reader should determine their storage practice and the length of time they are comfortable storing.

The FDA lets manufacturers mark their products with a date to help the seller determine how long to keep the item on the shelf and improve the buyer's use of the product at its best quality. Individual states can mandate dates, particularly on dairy products and eggs. Otherwise, dates are the manufacturer's "get the best taste now" date.

Foods that contain natural oils can go rancid or impact the taste. If you open a package of nuts and reseal them in the initial bag, they will grow stale or old more quickly than if you seal them in a canning jar or other seal-tight container.

The most extended possible storage times are represented below. Storage needs to be kept at normal room temperatures up to a high end of 83 degrees. The user needs to use airtight packaging. Even the best-preserved items will lose flavor and nutritional value over some time. Check your items in storage and rotate your items when needed.

I am prepared for the worst but will continue to hope for the best.

Six months: Most boxed food, fresh potatoes, granola, dried fruits, toaster pastries with fruit

One year: Many prepared foods can last this long, including cereals, rolled oats, nuts, candy, bottled dressings, mayonnaise, liquid vegetable oils, bottled juices, citrus juices, and canned citrus fruits. Commercially prepared Jerky is suitable for a year, but use homemade Jerky within several months. Additionally, preparers should use Home-canned foods within a year, but many will last longer. Remember to cook home-canned goods before use. Boil for 10 minutes for high-acid foods; 20 minutes for low-acid foods

Up to 18 months: High-acid canned goods such as tomatoes and vinegar-based products. Canned meats and most canned seafood (tuna, halibut, mackerel, shrimp), active dry yeast, chips/snacks, unshelled raw nuts, cake/ dessert mixes, teas, bottled juices, most spices/seasonings, jams and jellies, canned non-citrus fruits, pickles, and sauerkraut.

2 to 5 years: Beef and Chicken Bouillon cubes, white rice, powdered gelatin, white wheat flour, white flour pasta, tapioca, textured vegetable protein, hydrogenated peanut butter, ketchup, canned salmon and sardines, most dried fruits, and most low acid canned foods except meats, some fish and fruits, as well as sprouting seeds (alfalfa, soybean, wheat, etc.). Shelf-stable canned hams (usually 3 lbs. or less), stews, soups (non-tomato based), canned pasta, potatoes, corn, carrots, beans, peas, spinach, and pumpkin.

Up to 5 years: Processed (partially hydrogenated) liquid vegetable oils, Crisco shortening, cornmeal and corn flour, and nonfat powdered milk.

5 to 10 years: Most whole grains, dried legumes, dehydrated cheese, instant or vacuum-packed coffee, baking powder, powdered eggs, and frozen butter.

10 years or longer: Many basic spices and items for cooking have a naturally long shelf life, such as honey, sugar, soy sauce, apple cider vinegar, Worcestershire sauce, dried egg whites, and cocoa powder. Some of these products, especially Honey, have been known to last many years longer. Invest in higher quality items if you intend to keep these products on the shelf.

20 to 30 years: Freeze-dried foods.

Up to 30 years: Dried beans, dried apples, macaroni, dehydrated potato flakes, and oats in sealed, non-porous containers.

30 years or more: Use your Foodsaver bags to package whole-grain wheat and white rice to remove oxygen and keep stored at room temperature or below.

Forever: The following products will last forever if the items are correctly stored in sealed containers in cool, dry places. At the same time, it would still be best to rotate items and keep them as fresh as possible.

Baking soda (don't confuse baking powder) will last longer if sealed but will lose its *oomph* for baking. Liquor (vodka, whiskey, rum, brandy), Instant coffee, tea, salt, pepper, bouillon, and many herbs will keep indefinitely but may lose some taste. Cornstarch, used for making sauces, gravies, and soups instead of flour, is great for a gluten-free sauce and lasts longer. Also, it soothes sunburns and rashes.

Corn Syrup and **raw Honey** are common substitutes for sugar and sweetness. Honey can last forever! While ***Dried Beans*** have been previously listed as lasting for up to thirty years. Foods that can last for years and years may taste better when used earlier but are perfectly edible. Older beans will likely need extra soaking time, and adding baking soda to help the overnight soaking process will help.

Cans must exhibit a packing code to enable tracking of the product in interstate commerce and are used to locate products if there is a recall. It has nothing to do with the shelf life of a product.

Ramen Noodles were a favorite of people grabbing food for the pandemic. Many believe these may last forever, but you would probably like the taste better if eaten within five years.

Twinkies are another food rumored to last a lifetime, and if you want to prove that theory, go ahead. They will indeed last for years.

Food Storage Methods

Storage Buckets

Select Food Grade approved buckets! Add the sealable screw tops for sealing and easy removal of products. This lid has an O-ring gasket for tight snap-on around the outer edge of the bucket. The inner portion of the cover has a rubber gasket and screws tight to seal the bucket. Photos by M. Dillard

When preparing your storage buckets, fill them with items packaged for long-term storage; metal cans, glass jars, BPA-free plastic containers, and vacuum-sealed bags. Do not use pasta in cardboard boxes without sealing them in airtight containers.

Separate items into food groups for storage: meats in one, vegetables in another, and keep basics such as flour, sugar, oils, and spices together. It makes it easier to grab buckets for use. We cover lists of products to store later.

Vacuum Sealed Bags

Foods last longer when vacuumed-sealed as a normal process, especially when freezing meats. Vacuum-sealed bags will extend the life of stables such as flour, rice, beans, and more. They are much better than using plastic resealable bags, as all the air is removed, and the material holds up longer and is less porous. Placing these sealed bags in your food storage buckets for easy grabbing and going or staying put will provide extra protection.

Don't leave any food items in their original boxes without vacuum sealing. If the products are in cans or jars, they can be stored as packaged.

Canned Foods

Home canning has been a proven way to store food for long periods. It is a method of preserving food when placed in airtight, vacuum-sealed containers and heat-processed at 250°F (121°C). As the food cools, a vacuum seal prevents any new bacteria. This

process destroys microorganisms.

Photo by M. Dillard

The home canning process was the backbone of the American family for centuries. With the advent of commercial canning, the selection of prepared foods, and the frozen food process, the home canning industry decreased in the last forty years. However, with the resurgence in self-sufficiency, home, and organic gardening, the home canning process has increased in recent years.

The "mason" jar and heat-vacuum-sealed lid have remained the same since the 1800s. The water bath is for acidic foods, and use the pressure canning system for less acidic fruits and vegetables. The USDA Complete Guide to Home Canning is an excellent source for those interested in knowing the how-to of canning; the publication is at http://nchfp.uga.edu/publications/publications_usda.htm.

According to the USDA, Napoleon is considered "the father" of canning. He offered 12,000 French francs to anyone who could find a way to keep his troop's food supplies from spoiling. Chef Nicholas Appert received the prize after he invented the process of packing meat and poultry in glass bottles, corking them, and submerging them in boiling water. Without realizing it, he sterilized them, stopping bacterial growth.

Peter Durance patented metal containers for canning in 1810 in England. Englishman William Underwood migrated to Boston and established a canning plant in 1821, using tins for packaging his products.

Today the Underwood brand of Deviled Ham is still thriving, making this America's oldest canning company.

Canning, using metal cans versus jars, became the commercial method for preserving and selling food. Using chemical preservatives also created a longer shelf life for commercial products versus home-canned items. Living a healthy, no-preservative lifestyle is still possible with home canning.

When storing food for an emergency, cans versus breakable jars would be preferred for the possibility of travel. If your supply is for staying home, go for healthy home-canned goods.

The USDA advises that cans that are dented or bulging should be discarded. Also, heavily rusted cans may have tiny holes, allowing bacteria to enter. Surface rust that you can remove by rubbing with your finger is acceptable. If you open the cans and there is rust inside, do not eat the food. Rust (oxidized iron) is not safe to eat.

Expect the best; plan for the worse!

Dried and Cured Foods

Drying foods is the world's oldest approach to food preservation. Examples of dried foods are jerky, powdered milk, dried beans, dried fruits and vegetables, pasta, and rice. Solar or artificial heat drying can be as simple as spreading a layer of fruit or vegetables on trays for an extended period. Dehydrating meats is more complicated and requires cooking meats before drying to reach appropriate internal temperatures to avoid bacteria.

Curing meats or foods curbs the growth of microorganisms, as salt binds or removes water from the meat. Salt has been used for thousands of years as a critical food preservation item. Country hams, bacon, and other meats such as corned beef, salami, and pepperoni. Once they are cured, they become shelf-stable because they contain so little water that bacteria can't multiply. You still want to rotate your stores every few years to ensure taste and textures are always at their prime.

Freeze-dried foods are also made shelf-stable by using a commercial process to preserve foods using ice in a process known as sublimation or Flash freezing. When the foods are ready to be used, they are rehydrated like other dried foods by adding water. These foods then require packaging in moisture-proof, hermetically sealed containers.

Retort and MRE Packages

In relatively recent years, the traditional military-grade **M**eals **R**eady to **E**at have widened use and acceptance, thanks to the

retort pouch. This flexible packaging is lightweight and processed in a manner that sterilizes the food product to be shelf-stable. The old canned military C-Rations were transformed and became easier to carry, improving preservation and taste.

While retort packaging has improved its shelf life, these MRE products still have limitations. Like other foods, they store best and last longer in excellent, dry storage, and so do MREs. In a desert environment, with a constant temperature above 100°F, the food should be used within a month. Storing food at a cool 60°F can extend the shelf life to as long as seven years; depending on the product, this could be more.

Lt. Col. Rich Curry, 507th Air Refueling Wing at Tinker Air Force Base, wrote about the "unsung, lowly MRE." He provided facts about MREs as well as a few interesting asides:

- The thermal process used to create an MRE can be likened to canning in a pouch. It protects entrees and fruits, exposing the cooked meal to high heat and pressure, which kills any microorganisms that cause mold and spoiling.
- Oxygen and moisture are the two primary factors in food spoilage—the tri-laminate foil packaging results in a long MRE shelf life.
- MREs have approximately 1300 calories per meal, with 55% energy from carbohydrates, 35% from fat, and 15% from protein.

Lt. Col. Curry added a fact that is also useful for survival care, noting that using a pinch of instant tea from the MRE and applying the tea to your gums will help eliminate canker sores.

Root Cellar

The origins of the root cellar go back to before the days of refrigeration. However, it is still a viable option for storing many vegetables, particularly potatoes, onions, and the like. The cooler earth temperatures will remain cooler on hot summer days than the air temperature. The deeper the cold storage, the cooler your fresh vegetable will be and the longer they will last.

Chances are you don't live on a farm property or older area that often-had root cellars from years ago. A simple plan for keeping food in a container buried in your backyard will help preserve foodstuffs if you can ensure that the ground temperature will remain in the cooler range of good storage. Digging out an area big enough to place an old refrigerator or a large cooler and putting it so that there is an insulating cover to deter heat will work well.

You may also want to consider having food stored in an alternate location, such as another family member's home that is close by but far enough away to avert the same storm damage and power interruption. Just recognize that if the disaster is severe and long-term, the mentality of "everyone for themselves" will probably result in your food being grabbed by others.

"Organize, don't agonize."

When storing your food, make sure that you have containers packed and ready to go in the event you are driven to evacuate.

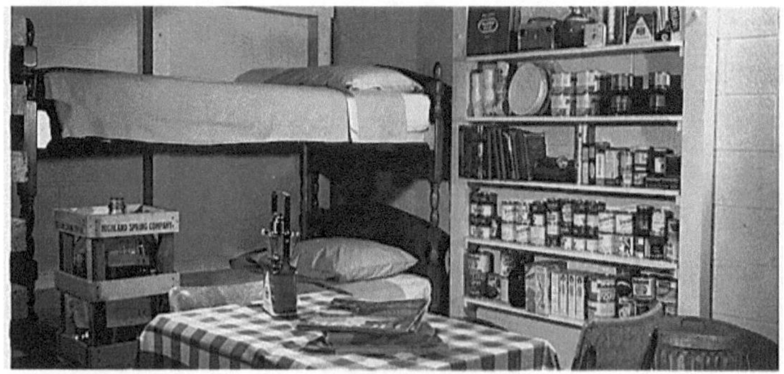

Family fallout shelter c. 1950, LOC Photos

Keep and mark the variety of food in each container; otherwise, you might grab and go with containers that only contain vegetables if you leave your home.

In the 1950 Fallout shelter photograph, all the cans are neatly organized on a shelf. It might have been handy for hiding out in a basement room waiting for the nuclear bombs to fall during the "Cold War," but not what we would need today.

What we need today is as essential as needing food for a prolonged period during their old cold war scare. Today, you would store your supplies in a basement or garage, any area that does not have extreme heat or cold shifts, and be ready for any peril, both at home and on the go. Keep your containers sealed and check your food stores several times a year. Keep your items fresh, rotated, and dated.

Don't forget your pets! Have a supply of food stored for your pets. Use the same guidelines for the quantity you use for your family. If you stockpile two weeks of food for yourself, ensure that your pet also has two weeks of food.

Photograph of a display of survival supplies for the well-stocked fallout shelter,

ca.1961. www.archives.gov

Planning Food Provisions

As you prepare your food stores, you must consider how many adults and children you will feed. Make sure you try to include family favorites and comfort foods when possible. Also, use foods that have a high nutritional value and meet the needs of the family, such as diabetic or allergic restrictions. You can try to store what you would typically use for two weeks.

When planning, you must ensure a minimum of one planned meal per day per adult, with more for children and pregnant women. Adding vitamins to your storage would be good if you have a filling but not the most nutritious meal. If you have a lot of dried foods that must be reconstituted, be sure to have extra water on hand too.

Don't rely on your favorite food place being open initially. Before the virus hit the US, many people took for granted going through a drive-thru fast-food chain or going out to lunch or dinner a couple of times and week. With the government shutting down all but essential businesses, people realized they needed more food than they usually buy.

For most of the country, we are six months into COVID-19 restrictions, and dining in is not an option at most places, or their capacity has been limited due to requirements to stay six feet apart for other people. If you can find an open restaurant, their menu is limited because resources are still limited. Different emergency types could also impact outside-of-the-home food sources, so plan accordingly.

TP hoarding explained.

Some people will be eating their own cooking for the first time in years

During the initial COVID-19 Pandemic in 2020, there were food shortages on an astonishing number of items as everyone tried to buy food and cleared out stores. Even six months after the virus began, there are still items that are hard to find, or limits remain on how much meat you can buy per grocery trip. I'm still searching for prime rib, beef brisket, rubbing alcohol, hand sanitizer, and a reasonable price on hamburger meat. Overall, food costs were up too.

Knowing what foods will keep the longest, having foods that will provide nutrition, and being items you plan to cook will keep you alive. However, having water is even more critical than food. Unless you intended to store water for drinking and cooking, you wouldn't last more than three days. More about water is given in the next section on staying home due to weather events.

Knowing what foods you can substitute for others is also something to consider. Instant dinner ideas such as Hamburger

Helper and other packaged meals were nowhere in sight, so people opened their cookbooks for the first time in years. Go ahead and think about those go-to meals you could make and what you would need now when you can find supplies.

Also, most cookbooks offer suggestions for substitutions; for example, if you don't have baking powder, how much baking soda could you use? If you don't have yeast for bread, there is a recipe that uses Mayo instead! It sounds crazy, but I made the rolls, and they were delicious. We have gotten used to everything ready-made or ready-to-mix, but you can use some old-fashioned recipes and substitutions in an emergency.

Stock Piling Other Items

Non-food items should be prepared and stored along with food and water stores. Having things kept and available with your other survival items will complete your preparations.

Most of these items I keep ready for camping anyway. Having them stored and ready for a weekend at the lake is no different than planning on having them for survival purposes at home, except my camping list includes a wine and beer opener!

A severe issue requiring you to stay at home and isolate requires items that are likely to be in short supply. Except for duct tape, all the below things were in short supply and almost impossible to find. Having them stored and ready for a shortage due to an event would add to your preparedness.

Other Items to consider:

Unscented chlorine bleach
Hand Sanitizer
Disinfectant Spray
Plastic/Latex/Vinyl Gloves
Alcohol and Hydrogen Peroxide – *both of these items are still in shortage six months after the COVID-19 pandemic*
Paper Products – *paper plates, paper towels, toilet paper*
Plastic Sealable Bags
Garbage Bags
Aluminum Foil
Soap – *Bath, Dish, and Laundry*
Duct Tape – *it has so many uses wherever you are*

Money *(ATMs might not work, or banks staffed due to COVID-19, there was a coin shortage, and some places wouldn't take anything but exact change.)*
Toilet Paper, Toilet Paper, Toilet Paper

It is usually wise to have the above items on hand anyway, but in an emergency, you will not be able to find most of these supplies!

When storing your miscellaneous items, you don't necessarily need to have 5-gallon watertight buckets for everything. A large footlocker-type container or a new trash can with a lid will work. Make the container size match the size of your family and the miscellaneous items stored.

Even the Big Box warehouse stores couldn't keep toilet paper and paper towels in stock, even with restrictions on purchase quantities.

Staying Home Due to Weather

In the event of a significant power outage while you are sheltering at home, you will need additional miscellaneous items. Conditions will require a heating, cooling, and water plan. If phone lines, internet, and cell service are interrupted, you need to know how to get help.

Long before any large-scale prepper movement began, having all the comforts of home available when waiting out a storm or on a camping trip seemed like the way to live life. Out-of-the-box thinking or innovation adds a few amenities or much-needed solutions; why avoid them?

Be Prepared! Preparing for emergencies or everyday life events isn't being paranoid, but it indicates that you are a planner and, even as an adult, follow the scout's model. Sometimes particular needs or circumstances in your life will give rise to a solution for an individual need that also makes sense in broader applications.

Winter, Spring, Summer, Fall- All year round, you should know what to expect

Summer storms do everything listed except snow and cold; instead, they can bring intense flooding and heat. Winter storms include many severe weather elements; high winds, freezing rain, sleet, heavy snowfall, and extreme cold. These elements result in blocked roads, downed power lines, communication outages, and accidents.

Know the Weather

Weather is unpredictable and can often deliver severe life-threatening events. Whether you are staying indoors or away from home when extreme weather hits, there are factors and tips you should consider for your family's well-being.

Certain storm types, such as Blizzards, are season-dependent; some storms are more likely during spring, others happen based upon conditions, and your family should be watchful year-round. Depending upon the area of the country where you reside, your storm preparations and the type of storms you are likely to encounter will vary.

Surviving winter storms at home or on the road requires preparation. As with other survival events, there are differences in preparing for either situation. Winter storms are usually forecasted with sufficient warning to activate your planning.

Weather forecasters can't be 100% accurate, and often forecasted storms are not as advertised. The prepared person will react to the potentially worse case rather than shrug off the possibility of yet another overly zealous and potentially wrong report. Notices of blizzards are provided well before storms, but the unknown is usually the amount of snow to expect.

We must expect everything possible to happen as we face everything.

Know these weather terms:

- ***Winter Storm Watch-*** *a hazardous winter storm is possible within the next 12 to 36 hours.*

- ***Winter Storm Warning-*** *a storm is occurring or is likely to occur within the next 12 hours, bringing snow of more than 6 inches, winds at 35 mph, and visibility of less than ¼ mile.*

- ***Blizzard Warning-*** *Sustained winds or frequent gusts of 35 miles per hour or greater with significant amounts of falling or blowing snow expected for 3 hours or longer.*

Weather factors such as wind and temperature will cause shifts in location and severity. Don't become complacent because predictions for your area often don't materialize.

Spring is a time of growing and replenishing nature, which can also bring an overabundance of spring rains. High watermarks from swollen creeks, streams, rivers, and lakes, whether in springtime or any time of the year, can be dangerous. In some areas of the country, melting snow can add to spring rain to increase flooding.

While flooding is considered a spring storm occurrence, it can happen at any time of the year, particularly in conjunction with Hurricanes, Tornadoes, and Thunderstorms. Being prepared for flooding and knowing the standard terms associated with the alerts from NOAA and FEMA can save lives:

- *__Flood Watch__ – Flooding is possible. Tune in to NOAA Weather Radio, commercial radio, or television for information*
- *__Flash Flood Watch__ – Flash flooding is possible. Be prepared to move to higher ground; listen to NOAA Weather Radio, commercial radio, or television for information*
- *__Flash Flood Warning__ – A flash flood is occurring; seek higher ground on foot immediately*

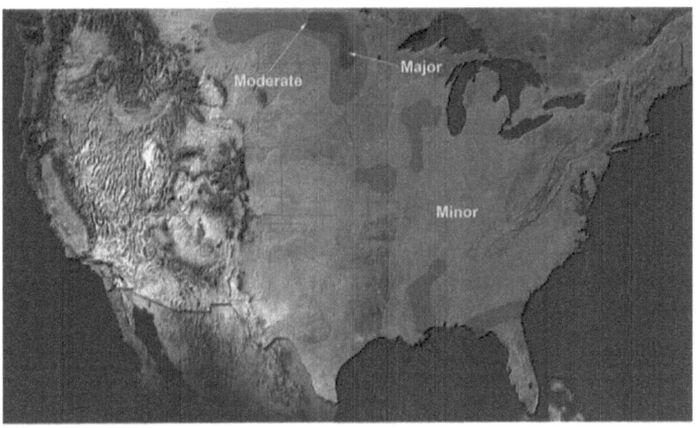

NOAA Spring Flood Model – usually published by March each year

Keep your emergency radio tuned to NOAA or a local station for weather updates.

Photo provided by NOAA

NOAA Weather Radio (NWR) All Hazards

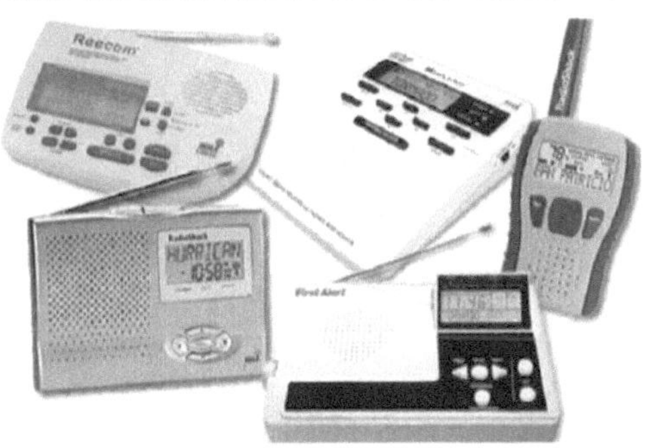

(www.weather.gov/nwr) Frequency 162.450 WNG736 nationwide

Making Life Easier

Besides the items on the various list of things to store for an emergency when staying home, these other items will be helpful. You may want to add specific details depending on your likes and needs. For example, if you are a coffee drinker, you will want to add a manual or camping-style coffee maker for when the power goes out or have plenty of instant coffee!

Garbage cans can make a practical storage container for the non-food items you should store. These containers do not seal well enough to keep underground or outside, but in your home, they are helpful. They are suitable for indoor storage, but each item in the can should be individually wrapped and sealed for additional protection.

The trash can concept and list of items to include is a documented concept published by government agencies for emergency preparedness. Customize the can to meet your family's emergency needs.

The items included below are items that I have needed to keep on hand due to significant weather situations in my area. Floods, downed trees, massive snowstorms, extended power outages, shortages in stores, if they were open, and more have helped define this list:

Hand/non-electric can opener
Battery Operated Radio *(keep batteries reversed until ready)*
Flashlight
Oil Lamps – *Keep a few placed around and keep extra oil in your container; I have a few on each level of the house*
Extra Batteries
First Aid Kit *(yes, we know you are at home but do you want to be stumbling in the dark looking for items, include a thermometer)*
Chemical Hand and Feet Warming packets
Chemical-activated ice packs for cooling
Nylon or Parachute Cord *(at least 20 feet)*
Camp Stove and Fuel *(store propane outside)*
Sterno - *a good cooking source and easy to store.*
Water Purification System/filters
Small tool kit
Lighters/Matches/Candles
Survival blanket
Foul Weather Gear
Portable AC/DC Charger
Phone charger - *if power is still available from your home or car, keep an extra on hand*
Generator

Power Options - Having a portable charger is a great device to have around the house for a multitude of reasons. Depending on your personal needs, you can think of all kinds of backup use for this device. In the case of short-duration power losses, the unit will charge phones, power fans, lower voltage medical equipment, or keep on a light. Features that are a must in any unit you consider:

- ☐ Power Booster cable for recharging car batteries
- ☐ AC/DC power Inverter (choose higher watts than you think you need, but at least 140W)
- ☐ DC Power jack for charging portable devices
- ☐ USB jack for charging electronics
- ☐ AC outlet (some units have more than one, which is nice)
- ☐ Built-in Flashlight
- ☐ AC charging cord (keep this unit plugged in, charged up, and ready to go at a moment's notice)

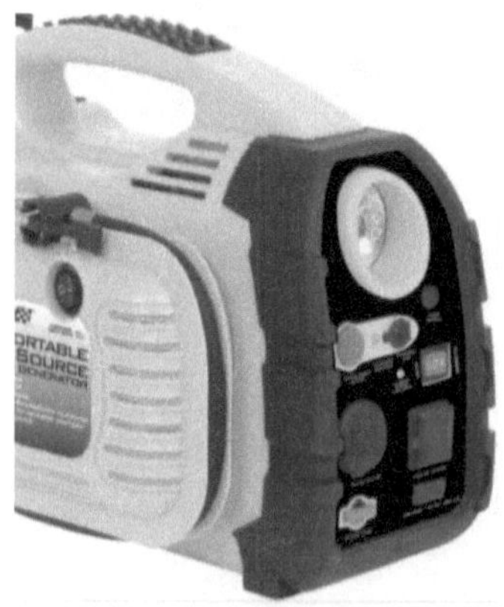

This Rally brand has some features that might be nice, but any brand will do if it has the features you want. This unit has a crank/pull start just in case you didn't keep the unit charged and *need to jump-start a car.*

Photo courtesy of Rally

Depending upon need and circumstances, having a couple of these handy would be helpful for everyday use. If you have someone in your home dependent upon nebulizers, alarms, or other medical devices, having some inverter and rechargeable power source is invaluable unless you have a large generator.

Look at your situation and think of the items that might make life a little easier or nicer if you were without power. Some things would be on the list that would be good if you were only without electricity for a few days. Some items would not be feasible for more extended outage periods as they would drain quickly.

If you live in an area as I do, the investment in a generator might be worthwhile to keep critical devices powered for a longer period, such as refrigerators, stoves, heat, etc.

Lighting can be in the form of battery-operated lights, flashlights, lanterns, candles, or, a favorite, the old-fashioned oil lamps. Oil lamps are easy to have around; they can be placed in most rooms, appearing as an accent piece but actually a prepper item placed in plain sight. Be sure to have various methods of lighting stored around the home and with your other prep supplies. Don't forget the fuel sources such as batteries and lamp oil.

Have lighting options available if the power is out

Don't forget about tools and items for outdoor use. Having a chain saw, extra fuel, and bar chain oil is always a good idea if you live in an area with large trees that would come down in a major storm. A tow rope or chain would be useful to pull trees out of the road, drive, or away from your home. Keep these items in their usual place.

Water

Suppose you are stuck in your home and have water available; not a problem. But if your power goes out and you are on a well, you need alternate power or have water on hand. It is best to remember that in the event of a major disaster, the "taps won't run," so water won't flow if utilities are out due to weather or other disruptions.

You must have more water than you do food. Whether at home or on the road, you must plan to have water for each person in your group. If you grab a bag and go, consider how much water you will require to reconstitute your dried foods and drinking water.

Your plan should include about 6 gallons of water per week/per person for drinking. If you have pets, allow 1 quart per day for each dog or cat. Because water is so plentiful and easy to obtain by simply turning on a faucet, preppers often think they will have time to find water. Being left high and dry because you didn't allow enough time to store water is unnecessary.

While portable water purification is a must for being mobile, it is still a good idea for home use. When planning to survive at home, storing large quantities of water is more manageable, unlike outdoors. It is especially true if you are a procrastinator and don't store enough water.

You don't miss your well until the water runs dry

Anything can happen to cut off your water supply at any time. Even a minor storm or temporary water shutoff can be frustrating and inconvenient. Not having water available at all can be deadly.

As we saw with the unexpected COVID-19 virus, bottled water evaporated from the shelves.

Water that has gone bad due to improper storing or a poor choice of container is also deadly. Filling a large drum with water and then sticking it in a corner to age is not safe. Water needs to be purified and changed out at regular intervals.

The quality of water that goes into your containers must be considered. Most public water systems test the water in their locality, and the water should be acceptable for storing. If you are on private water or a well system, you should consider purchasing bottled water for storage.

Most water treatment systems and purification processes effectively treat many types of contaminants. Even chlorine treatment may not remove bacteria that can make your family ill. However, when planning to store water for a long time and with the water source being so critical, don't take a chance that private supply water will be safe.

"Here's a rule of life: You don't get to pick what bad things happen to you."

If you are storing water as cheaply as possible, ask friends or family on public water systems to let you fill your bottles at their homes. Don't worry about filling all your containers at one time. Just as you rotate food, you should rotate your water stores. Either buying water a little at a time to store or hitting the tap regularly to save water will work.

Selecting a Water Container

As crucial as water is to your survival, you should ensure that your water storage plan keeps drinking water as pure as possible. Under optimum conditions, you can store water for about five years. That means that you can't reuse old milk containers or soda bottles. You also can't keep your water in direct sunlight, where the heat will help bacteria "nasties" grow.

How bad can the water you are storing be? After all, you drink this water daily and don't treat the water. You drink fresh water every day, not water that has been stored for years!

Storing water in recycled containers is only suitable for non-potable sources for flushing toilets, washing clothes, and bathing. Washing empty soda bottles, milk jugs, juice containers, and large buckets and pails with lids are excellent choices for building a cache of non-drinking water. These bottles or jugs may still have residual "leftovers" from their original liquid.

Re-using those old containers is a very cheap and easy way to put aside water, don't drink the water. Finding an easy and inexpensive way to store drinking water is more important.

When buying your drinking water containers, there are several vital points to consider:

- Food-grade plastic (BPA-free) or glass containers with tight-fitting screw-on caps, unbreakable containers are best

- [ ] Sturdy containers that will hold up to a prolonged storage period
- [ ] No metal containers

RV or camping-style portable water containers are a great choice and inexpensive.

When you have stored your water, you may still need to purify the water later. One of the most straightforward processes for purifying water is using Clorox bleach! Of course, the bleach should not have any cleaners or soap additives.

More is not better when adding Chlorine to your water to retard algae and bacteria growth. The North Carolina Extension Service recommends the following ratios:

- [ ] Four drops of bleach per quart or liter container of water
- [ ] 8 drops bleach per 2-quart, 2-liter, or ½ gallon container of water
- [ ] 16 drops bleach, or 1/4 teaspoon, per gallon or 4-liter container of water

Even though you tried to ensure that your water was clean and pure and you added bleach, you can't foresee the condition your water may be in five years from now. Like the Boy Scouts, you should always be prepared and have a large pot handy for boiling water.

Additionally, the stored water can develop a flat or musty taste with or without the bleach. To improve the taste of water, pour the water from one clean container to another. Do this several times to aerate the water, making it taste better. It is the exact process you use when aerating older wine, this won't turn your water into wine, but it will taste fresher!

You might not know what you may face, so be prepared to withstand almost anything

Hopefully, you will have the room and the means to store a plentiful enough water supply. If your stored water isn't enough, you can use the most overlooked water in your home, the Hot Water Tank! Turn on the faucets and fill as many containers as possible for your other uses. As soon as your water stops flowing due to a major storm or event, shut off the water valve coming into your home to prevent tainted water from coming into the house.

Your water heater holds the largest concentration in your home, anywhere from 35 to 50 gallons. Ensure you turn the electricity or gas off to the water heater, even if the power source is out. The water heater would be damaged if it was empty and the power returned.

You can open the drain at the bottom of the tank and turn on a hot-water faucet. If you connect a hose to the tank outlet, make sure that the hose is a water-grade RV hose, not a garden hose. You will get the same quality of water you usually have in your home for drinking.

As a young child, I remember my parents filling sinks and bathtubs with water in the event of a major storm warning for extreme cold (frozen pipe potential) or tornado (loss of power and water). This water was non-potable, meaning that it was meant for flushing toilets, washing hands, etc. But not for drinking!

Filling pitchers and jugs with water for drinking was a separate duty. The expectation that pipes may break or storms could interrupt or taint our drinking water had us preparing for several days of the outage. Today, it is easy to buy and store bottled water for drinking and cooking for several days during an outage.

Heating and Cooking at Home

Extreme cold can cause several safety concerns, including frostbite, hypothermia, carbon monoxide poisoning, fires (from alternative heating sources), and a few items for your survival kit.

Dress appropriately, and wear several layers of loose-fitting, lightweight, warm clothing rather than one layer of heavy clothing. Wool clothing will help wick moisture away from your body and is optimal when exposed to cold temperatures, as it retains almost 80 percent of its insulating ability.

If you venture outside, stay dry and in wind-protected areas. Wear mittens and a hat, and cover your mouth with a scarf to protect your lungs. Watch for signs of frostbite and hypothermia when exposed to the cold. With frostbite, your skin appears white and waxy, with numbness or no feeling in that area. Hypothermia includes shivering, numbness, confusion, dizziness, stumbling and weakness, slow or slurred speech, and shock.

When a person's body temperature drops to 95°F/35°C, the person is in the primary stage of hypothermia. If the body isn't warmed, the heart and other organs must work harder and eventually fail. It is essential to keep your body temperature at an average of 98.6°F/37°C.

Medical attention is needed for frostbite and hypothermia. Interim steps you can take using your survival kit to avoid or assist with issues include using your chemical warming packs, survival blanket, and extra blankets in the home. Additionally, you can use blocks or rocks to heat the person. If you notice any of these signs, take the person's temperature. If it is below 95°, attention is needed.

When medical care is not available, you must provide warmth. Warm the person's core, chest, neck, head, and groin with hot beverages if they are alert, or use an electric blanket or heating pad if they are not alert. If you are without power, using person-to-person or skin-to-skin contact under loose, dry layers of blankets, clothing, towels, or sheets will also help.

Tip: Heating rocks and placing them near the person, not in direct contact, will create warmth under blankets to help keep the victim warm.

After body temperature has increased, it is crucial to keep the person dry and wrapped in a warm blanket, including their head and neck. A person with severe hypothermia may also be unconscious and not seem to have a pulse or be breathing. CPR should be provided while trying to warm the person.

Besides keeping everyone warm, be prepared to use alternate cooking if impacted by a significant weather event. If your home has a fireplace, make sure you keep a store of wood available year-round that will last several weeks or longer when used for heat.

A cozy-looking fireplace during everyday living becomes a lifesaving heat or cooking source in a power outage. When needed, a wood-burning fire heat can be a

direct or indirect heat source. Hundreds of years ago, the fireplace was the primary heat and cooking source, and if it would work for our forefathers, we could make it work for ourselves in a pinch. The more wood you can store, the better since you can use wood cords for heat and cooking. Having an extra grate to put in the fireplace makes cooking work.

If you don't have a fireplace, don't use fire indoors as the smoke needs to be vented. Not having a fireplace doesn't mean you can't have a heat and cooking source; it just takes a little more work.

When trying to outlast a terrible storm or disaster, your ability to cook and keep warm is a priority. While wood-burning fires can provide cooking and heat, a more regulated temperature is possible using a propane grill or steno cans. Have a plan for sustaining your family without power: no microwave, stove/oven, toaster, or other appliances on which you usually depend.

A camp stove or propane burner typically intended for camping use is an excellent addition to your home survival kit. Most people have outdoor grills or fire pits in their yards for cozy evenings. Those fire pits can be a great source if your yard isn't flooded or you don't have a blizzard. Place a grate or metal rod across your fire pit to help with cooking, as multiple pots and pans can be used simultaneously.

- If you lose power and foods require refrigeration, placing the items in the newly fallen snow will keep them frozen

Grate from a fireplace, grill shelves, racks from your oven, get inventive; this is not the time to stop thinking and doing...you will be surprised how you can prove the idea that "necessity is the mother of all invention."

It is easy to create an outdoor cooking area and even a possible way to create a limited amount of warmth. Using a fireplace grate, an outdoor grill grate, or any metal rack placed over a fire will create a cooking method for use outdoors.

Putting concrete blocks on the grate of an outdoor fire to heat them and then moving them into your home on another grate will release some heat to provide little radiant heat. Blocks placed at the foot of the bed will provide some heat for the bed, similar to the old -fashion method of bed warming. You will want to place these on a metal or non-flammable base to ensure the heat doesn't start any low flash point fires.

A bed warmer or pan was a common item before indoor heat, particularly in areas with frigid winters. A metal, lidded skillet-looking container would be filled with coals or hot rocks. The container would then be placed under the covers of the bed to warm the bed. In the event of a significant power loss during the coldest months of the year, old remedies are potential solutions. Use cast iron skillets if you have them for this purpose.

An easier solution is to have propane or kerosene heaters. Having used both in an emergency power outage has kept my family warm, but you need to have a large enough area that the fumes are not overpowering. Keep a portable Carbon Monoxide unit in your home, like an RV monitor. The monitor will tell you if unhealthy levels are in your alternative heated area.

Using all your extra blankets, including sleeping bags, you should have everyone sleep together for warmth. Close off rooms you don't need and keeping people together in one area will help contain heat. Seal off drafty doors and windows.

In the event you lose power and foods require refrigeration, placing the items in the newly fallen snow will keep them frozen

Thinking like a Boy Scout or Brownie can provide helpful solutions to make the best of your unfortunate situation. Meat can be wrapped in aluminum foil and cooked on your car's engine. Hobo stew can be easily fixed over a campfire. These were both scouting tricks for surviving.

Thinking and acting like a scout is admirable in everyday life but even more favorable in crises to ensure you keep warm and eat well. The Scout motto - Be Prepared- summarizes the thinking needed in a survival mindset. "Be Prepared in Mind by having disciplined yourself to be obedient to every order, and also by having thought out beforehand any accident or situation that might occur, so that you know the right thing to do at the right moment, and are willing to do it."

**Being ready for the Storm can mean the difference between life and death,
or, at the very least, comfort and cold.**

Keeping Cool

Just as you must plan to keep warm, you also must ensure you avoid heat exhaustion if you stay in place and have no cooling. Stay in a sheltered area for extreme heat and use fans or air conditioning to keep cool. Be sure to keep an eye on pets, too, making sure you and your pets are drinking plenty of water. Be aware of the symptoms of heat stroke, exhaustion, and heat cramps. Heatstroke can easily lead to death!

The human body can quickly succumb to heatstroke and dehydration when more water leaves the body than is taken in.

Symptoms of dehydration—
- Impaired thinking and mental acuity
- decrease in urination
- dry mouth and throat
- dizziness when standing up

You lose water naturally through breathing, perspiration, urine, and bowel movements. For your body to function properly, you must supply liquids by consuming beverages and foods containing water. When high heat overheats your body and your core body temperature rises above 104 degrees Fahrenheit, you are experiencing a cooling malfunction.

Our bodies respond to heat by using perspiration to reduce our body's temperature. The elderly and infants are most inclined to experience heatstroke, but we are all susceptible.

"Even seasonal situations can bring with them lessons that last a lifetime."

When you become overheated, there are three progression points: heat cramps, heat exhaustion if you have not been able to cool down, and heat stroke. Drinking plenty of fluids, staying inactive during the hottest period of the day, and finding a cool spot to rest will usually stop the progression of heat-related illness. Keeping wet towels on your head and neck will help.

Heatstroke, when left untreated, can be fatal, but it doesn't need to result in death. Ensure sunscreen is applied when going outside and, if possible, stay indoors during the peak heat of 10 AM to 3 PM.   Also, wear light-colored, loose-fitting, and lightweight clothing. A hat and a handkerchief for soaking in water and placing them behind your neck are also valuable items.

If you have a fan that is battery-powered or a power pack that can run a fan, place a pan of water in front of the fan, and it will blow colder, reducing your body temperature faster.

Know the signs and symptoms of heat-induced illness:

- Hot, red, and dry skin- chapped and cracked lips too
- Strong, rapid pulse
- Headache/Dizziness – often the early signs
- Hyperventilation
- Confusion
- Nausea
- Seizures
- Hallucinations or unconsciousness

When traveling, ensure you have plenty of drinking water and a five-gallon jug in case your car overheats. If you sit in an overheated vehicle, you will likely become overheated too.

The issue of dehydration and heat exhaustion while staying in your home is a genuine concern, possibly more critical during a heat-related event than a cold-weather one. When waiting out an event during the summer heat, it is vital to keep it as cool as possible. Having windows open to create cross-drafts might help.

When your home is flooded, move to the highest level to wait for help or until the water recedes.

Communication Signals at Home

Depending on the event type, you may still be able to use your landline or cell phone for communication. In other circumstances, normal communication modes may be unusable, from severe weather to a more serious threat. Besides, the internet and texting could be non-existent. For people over 40 years old, the idea that texting and even cell service might not be available would be inconvenient but not life-stopping. Younger generations have been brought up on cell phones and always have available services.

As we have seen in recent disasters such as Hurricane Katrina, a large-scale event can bring down conventional communications. Cell towers are destroyed, internet servers are brought down, telephone poles for landlines are snapped like twigs, and we are left unable to call for help.

Having an amateur radio or "ham" radio would be a viable means of communication, but most people either don't have the equipment or the knowledge. The use of amateur radio requires having an FAA license. Study guides for the test and a minimal equipment investment would be worthwhile if you are located in a remote area for that "just in case" circumstance. While I had a license, I no longer

relied on Ham radio. Cell service has spoiled us all.

Having a shortwave radio for listening to broadcasts from NOAA Weather Radio (NWR) (Frequency *162.450)* will keep you abreast of critical incoming alerts but won't provide you with outgoing communication. We might not be able to get all our news and weather from our smartphones.

NWR broadcasts official Weather Service warnings, watches, forecasts, and other hazard information 365 days a year. NWR reports on more than weather conditions, covering environmental (chemical and oil spills) and public safety matters and infrastructure outages.

A shortwave radio that covers multiple bands from marine, FM, AM, and several SW bands can be purchased. In addition to weather reports, SW radio will have news reports from numerous sources from around the globe. The incoming news feeds will help you be prepared and indicate the severity of the event and the efforts made to support the public.

Since you likely lost all outbound commutations, your ability to use the wilderness survival markings and symbols is equally essential in a homebound event. Having visible signals to let someone know that you and your family have remained in your home could be crucial. Just as in the wild, signs can be used for your home to communicate your presence and need for help. Use the Standard Civil Symbols for rescue on your roof for easy visibility. The V and X symbols are the most likely to be needed.

Some people will use paint on the roof, particularly in flooded regions. Use the same signs to mark open field areas when out in the wild, in the available yard, and in road areas at your home.

 V- Requires assistance

X- Needs medical help

N- means no

Y- means yes

Signaling is even more important if you require assistance if your home is in a remote area or away from an urban or suburban neighborhood. Hopefully, your sustainment supplies will provide everything you and your family need, and outside aid won't be a critical issue.

The roof would work for signaling since there is no way a fire can be used.

Photo by K. Connors

Cache Storage

Your "survival cache" doesn't need to be large to be an effective solution. Surviving in your home might need a watertight spot for copies of important papers, or staying at home may not be entirely viable due to storm damage or the need to evacuate. Having a couple of stored cache locations at your home, a relative's, or a place along an evacuation route could be a lifesaver.

The cache doesn't need to hold everything, just some critical survival items. Using a waterproof container that is easily buried or hidden and quickly found is the priority for your cache. The containers should be in an area and location you will promptly recognize and find. Under optimal conditions, when a situation dictates that your home is unsafe, you should have the time to grab your to-go bag containing items needed for outdoor survival.

Bury multiple pipe caches together or separately. Your supply can contain money, a first aid kit, a fire-starting kit, a compass, a knife, a handgun, ammo, duct tape, a poncho, snacks, purification water tablets, personal medications, or supplies. Container size will depend upon your supply list; however, a 4" or 6" diameter PVC pipe of a length that you determine gives you storage flexibility.

"Preparation time is never wasted time."

You create an easy and simple cache from PVC pipes cut to lengths you want and put caps on the ends. Another simple but effective container can be a waterproof, sealable five-gallon food-grade bucket with a seal/gasket lid. The buckets require digging bigger holes and are more difficult to find than making the simple pipe cache.

PVC Pipe Cache Components:

PVC pipe, PVC End Cap, PVC drain cleanout plug, PVC drain adapter, and PVC cement are all available at your local hardware store.

Cutting the pipe to the required length, applying the cement to the tube, and placing the end cap items on each end will create a durable 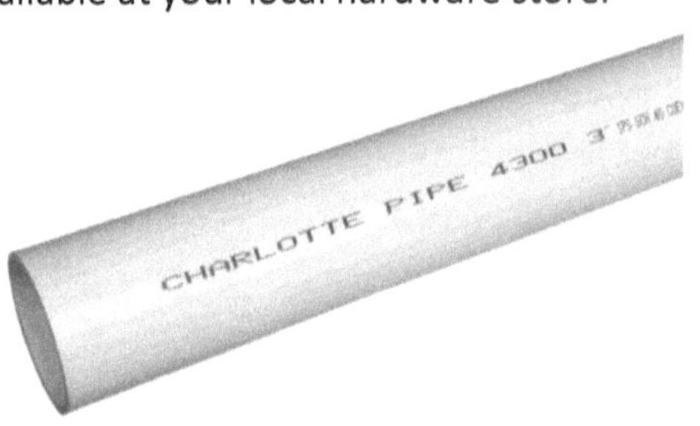 storage option. Make sure the pipe and end caps are fully sealed by making the cement cover the entire outside diameter of the pipe where the cap will fit.

Use the solid end cap to glue to one end of the pipe. This end will not be removable. If you want access to both ends of the tube, you can use the adapter and screw cap.

Glue the adapter to the open end of the PVC pipe, leaving the threaded end ready to receive the drain cap for your storage access point.

If you don't want to make your own, you can find people that have made the tubes and sell them at gun shows, flea markets, and even online. Making your tubes is quick and easy and can fit what you want to store.

Cache tubes aren't just for burying in the yard but can be used to pack and store supplies in cars, boats, and homes. A tube takes up very little space but can be loaded with needed items.

Having a tube in your trunk or under your seat is a great way to be prepared for inclement weather, as well as a bug-out supply kit. Possible supplies for including in your car tube:

- Snacks – Trail Mix, Crackers, Energy Bars, Peanut Butter, Bottles of Water, Mints
- Tools – Flashlight, Glow Sticks, Multi-Tool (pliers, screwdriver, wrench), Hammer, Compass, Flares, Nylon Cord, Duct Tape, Gloves, Matches, Poncho, Sewing Kit
- First Aid – Tape, Antiseptic, Aspirin (or fever reducers), bandages, Cotton Balls, Alcohol, Dental Floss, Hand Sanitizer, Sunscreen, Lip Balm, and Insect Repellent

Tips: Alcohol-soaked cotton balls are also good fire starters! Dental Floss works as a string, fishing line, and thread.

Weather Events

If you are on a road trip when a weather event happens or if you deliberately need to leave your home, be prepared to survive the event. There are a lot of different scenarios, ranging from major winter blizzards to all sorts of storms: floods, tornados, hurricanes, wildfires, and more.

This section will deal with natural disasters due to weather and how you might prepare yourself. There is some specific planning, dependent upon the time of year and the area in which you live. Additionally, if you can't remain in your home, you need your emergency supply list items (Making Life Easier, pg. 46) or a smaller travel kit we will address.

Any of the following weather situations can create a situation of personal peril. Knowing the types of storms, you can encounter and what the storm may bring helps you prepare and plan. You can survive weather issues if you know what to expect and are ready. The first step is to know the weather, and then we will look at surviving outdoors.

Winter Blizzard

Blizzards occur, and if you must travel or leave your home due to a weather event, you should be actively monitoring storm and road conditions. Weather deterioration can happen quickly, but hopefully, you followed the weather before heading out.

Photo Courtesy of FEMA

Unless you live in a climate that never receives snow during winter months, your car should contain a Winter Storm kit.

Photo Courtesy - Ready Wisconsin readywisconsin.wi.gov

Depending on the space you have in your vehicle, you may choose to use a plastic tote filled with the essentials or a small Cache tube. The climate zone that you live or travel in will influence your choice. The more severe the weather zone, the more robust the kit.

"Purpose without preparation is meaningless." — Andrena Sawyer

NOAA suggests that the following items be at the ready for a foray into winter weather:

- ☐ A vehicle that is fully fueled and winterized
- ☐ Blankets/sleeping bags
- ☐ Flashlight with extra batteries

- ☐ High protein/calorie, non-perishable food, MREs, snack crackers, trail mix, peanut butter
- ☐ Tool/Safety Kit
  - o Knife
  - o Multi-tool or Hammer, pliers, screwdriver
  - o Water-proof matches or fire-starting kit
  - o Nylon/Paracord rope
  - o Shovel
  - o Jumper cables
  - o Windshield scraper
  - o Sand/ cat litter or, better yet, tire chains
  - o Tow rope
  - o Emergency markers/flares/ flags, glow sticks
- ☐ Extra clothing, gloves, boots, socks, and a winter cap

These items should be in your car throughout the winter "just in case." You never know when your car could break down, slide off the road, or have trees block your path.

Suppose you become stranded while in your vehicle; the first rule of safety is to remain in your car! You can run your engine for about ten minutes every hour to provide heat. Be sure that your exhaust pipe is clear to avoid carbon monoxide poisoning.

Before traveling, a travel plan should have been left with a friend or relative. Making yourself more visible when stranded is essential. If you run off the road, turn on your dome light at night when running your engine. Tie a piece of orange or brightly colored cloth to your car antenna or a nearby tree.

Preparation Prevents Poor Performance

When the storm is over, you may be unable to dig your car out, so your priority remains your safety and rescue. Remind yourself to follow the sustainment rules in wilderness survival. Find a dry shelter, build a fire, and create signals for recovery. If you must leave the vehicle, place a note with your name, phone number,

and address and put it in plain sight on your dash. Note which direction you are heading to make it easier for rescue workers to assist in your safety.

Here are a few special tips for cold-weather survival:

- Do not eat snow, as it lowers your body temperature. You can melt the snow to provide drinking water.
- Before sleep, eat, and urinate - your body needs the digestive process to help keep you warm, and your body won't work as hard to stay warm if your bladder isn't full
- Preventing hypothermia is important; keeping your head, neck, and extremities warm is critical to stop your body from shifting blood flow to your limbs, where it can become more quickly cooled

- Fleece and wool garments and blankets will wick moisture and provide warmth
- Don't overexert from pushing a car, shoveling, or other taxing exercises; not only could this cause a heart attack, but it can overheat your body and lead to hypothermia

"No matter how prepared you are you're never ready; however, you've minimized what you could"

Flooding

While flooding is considered a spring storm occurrence, it can happen at any time of the year, particularly in conjunction with Hurricanes, Tornadoes, and Thunderstorms.

Taking weather alerts seriously prevents fatalities, most of which occur when people try to drive through floodwaters and are swept away. Thirty-nine percent of flood-related deaths are related to driving. Seventy-one percent of flood deaths are males.

Do you know these Flood Facts?

- Hydroplaning causes steering and braking control loss when a thin layer of water prevents direct contact between tires and the road, runway, or another surface. Severity depends upon tire wear, speed, and road surface.

- Do not use your cruise control during heavy rains, as the car's effort to keep your speed consistent will keep your wheels turning, and you will have a delayed reaction to hydroplaning.
- Just six inches of water will reach the bottom of most passenger cars and impact steering control, and possibly cause your engine to stall, rendering further control issues.
- A heavy vehicle will float away in a foot of water, and two feet of swift-moving water will sweep vehicles away, even large SUVs (Sport Utility Vehicles) and pick-up trucks.

FEMA photo credit

FEMA offers the following guidelines when dealing with flood areas:

- Stay tuned to your radio and television for the latest information, and immediately move to higher ground if you are in an affected area
- Be aware and avoid streams, drainage channels, canyons, tunnels, and other areas prone to flooding in your area

- Have pre-planned routes for evacuation, do not try and cross moving water or drive through water of unknown depth
- If you must evacuate, make sure to take your stocked "grab bags or buckets," secure your home, shut off power, bring in outdoor furniture, move items of significant importance to the upper floor or attic of your home

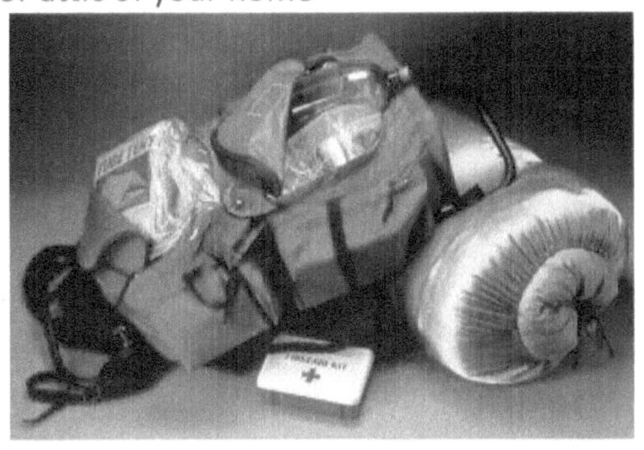

- Do not return home until reports advise that the roads and areas allow safe travel —weakened bridges and roadways are dangerous, as well as downed power lines
- When you do return home, remember-
    - drinking water is not immediately safe
    - flood water contains chemical, biological and waste-hazards
    - structural damage may be present but hidden from view

Floods not created by man-made failures such as failed dam systems and melting mountain snow result from an overabundance of rain. Sometimes it is not the amount but how quickly the rain falls and the ability of the ground to soak in the rainwater.

Unusual periods of prolonged or frequent rain can overwhelm the ground's ability to absorb the new or existing water, which causes water spillage over the banks of streams and lakes.

Thunderstorms, or thunder-boomers as we called them as children growing up, are beautiful to watch but are quickly dangerous. Major rainstorms have the added visual and sound effects of big booms and flashes of lightning. The booming sound of thunder clapping, and the crack of the lightning, are awe-inspiring. So too, is the damage that can be left behind.

"Don't touch the screen door," was a familiar shout from my parents as I would watch thunderstorms with lightning in Oklahoma. Sometimes you could feel the charge of the storm and be sure it would jump out and tag you. I was also admonished to stay off the phone and away from electrical appliances.

Thunderstorms

Credit: NOAA Photo Library, NOAA Central Library; OAR/ERL/NSSL [nssl0016], Norman, Oklahoma

As with all weather events, your local climate and location determine the significance of these Thunderstorms. Some parts of the county experience more frequent storms. The topography of an area also impacts related events. For example, those Oklahoma thunderstorms quickly created flash floods.

Flash floods are dangerous and pose a high likelihood of injury or death. One minute you might be driving down a street when a thunderstorm approaches, and the amount of rain quickly runs off the dry ground; storm sewers become clogged with too much water too fast, and water surges. Be prepared to find high ground in a well-protected shelter.

- More people die every year from lightning that every thunderstorm produces.

- Thunderstorms are considered severe if hail of at least 1 inch in diameter is present or if the storm includes wind gusts of 58 miles per hour or more.

- The combination of lightning, hail, winds, and rain create widespread havoc: lost power, structural damage, and crop losses, and result in a significant financial impact on the economy.

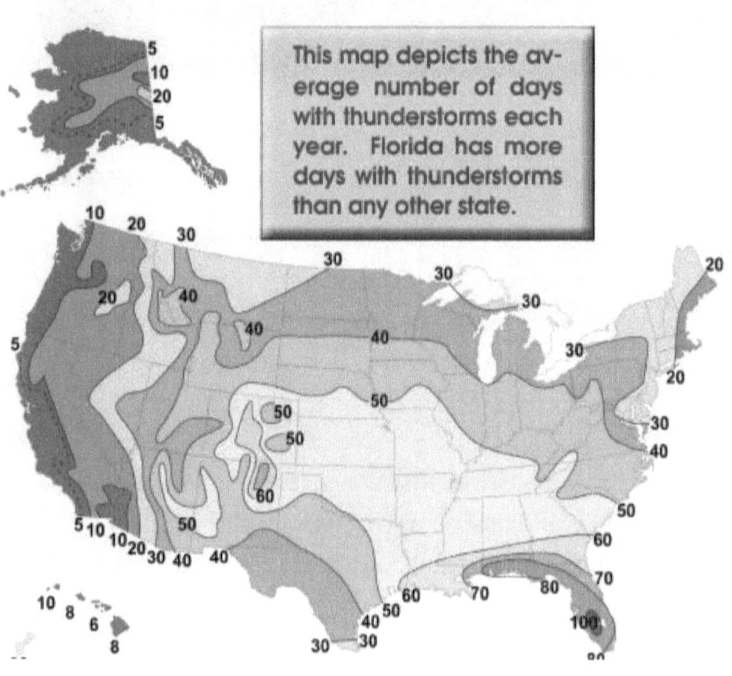

Tropical Storms, Cyclones, Hurricanes, and Tornadoes – Oh My!

Winds, rain, and damages are all expectations of these significant storm types, which are some of **nature's most powerful and destructive phenomena.** We all know the quote, "Toto, we aren't in Kansas anymore," and the images of tornado winds swirling around in the Wizard of Oz. What you may not realize is the similarity of the different wind events of cyclones, hurricanes, tornadoes, and tropical storms and the severity of their impact on property and life.

NOAA classifies these windy storms by wind strength or force. Storm watches are issued 48 hours before the storm to allow preparation and evacuation planning; warnings give you less time.

- **Hurricane watch** – winds of 74 mph or higher expected within 48 hours

- **Tropical Storm/Cyclone watch** - winds of 39 to 74 mph

- **Tornado watch** – conditions are in place to create tornados; winds can range from 30mph to 200 mph

Once a warning is issued, evacuation plans should be executed; **warnings expect the storm to begin within the hour**. Storm effects include heavy rainfall, high water from storm surges, rising rivers, high winds, and poor visibility, and tropical storms can spawn tornadoes as they move inland.

Severe wind storm events can happen at any time of the year; however, conditions must come together to create "the perfect storm." Atlantic hurricane storms usually begin in June and occur during the next six months, with a peak in August through October. Pacific hurricanes also run from June through

November, with peak seasons lasting from July through September.

Photo Credit- FEMA

Whether impacted by a tropical storm or an inland wind event, it is wise to have your grab bag, food, water, and emergency equipment- generators, battery-powered gear, cell phones, and radio prepared and ready! Coastline safety requires knowing safe inland evacuation routes away from the storm and coastline. It is imperative to know the locations of official storm shelters.

Keeping your home prepared in areas with heavy wind and rainstorms is a significant preventive step to protecting your family and your property. Steps to take to prepare your home before you evacuate include:

- Window shutters or plywood cover windows to prevent breakage and rain damage.
- Keep trees trimmed near your home's windows and check large trees near your roofline
- Ensure that gutters and downspouts are clear so that rainwater will not back up under eaves   by destructive winds, tornadoes, and flooding from these
- Bring in or tie down patio and lawn furniture, trash cans, breakable garden art, etc.

Tornadoes most often occur with thunderstorms and can result from hurricanes, usually well away from the center eye of the initial storm.   These tag-along tornadoes are generally weaker than the primary cyclone.

An angry-looking tornado funnel in Texas, 1995

Credit: NOAA Photo Library, NOAA Central Library; OAR/ERL/NSSL [nssl0179]

A tornado is a violent swirling air funnel, reaching down from the clouds to the ground.   Unlike their cousins, the hurricane and tropical storms, tornadoes can occur at any time of the year.   While the tornado usually moves from southwest to northeast, these violent storms can suddenly move in a swift direction.

The swirling funnel can cut a wide swath; reports of past storms have had the funnel making a path of more than 2 miles wide. The more debris picked up and swirled around in the funnel, the darker and angrier the storm appears.   Be ready year-round, but be especially vigilant when your weather is warm, rainy, or humid and windy.

When tornado watches and warnings are issued, don't become lulled into a sense of safety and well-being because the winds have calmed. "The calm before the storm" doesn't mean the storm has passed; as long as the warning is in effect, take cover. Have your grab bag ready and your plan for protecting your family in place.

Other Weather Happenings

Tropical storms, tornadoes, and thunderstorms bring plenty of rain and create havoc, but extreme summer heat and lack of rain bring drought and potential wildfires. Not enough rain can create dangerous conditions that require your awareness and preparedness.

While drought isn't going to cause you to flee your home, unlike the 1930s Dustbowl that displaced thousands of people, drought conditions make wildfires a real danger. Even if your home area doesn't suffer from drought and potential wildfire, when traveling, you should be aware of reports of droughts and fires.

Having an emergency kit in your car for a just-in-case travel problem can help you keep ahead of trouble. If you know what to expect before and during an emergency, you are on the critical path to success. Having your plan in place can make all the difference between being prepared and saving crucial minutes in your bug-out plan.

Remember the phrase, "if it's predictable, it's preventable!" Awareness and preparation can mean the difference between life and death in natural and man-made disasters.

Know the types of weather hazards you are likely to encounter, and having your resources tucked away may not protect you, but your chances are greatly improved.

Whether the weather is in one of the previously discussed events or other events such as earthquakes, mudslides, avalanches, Derechos, and weather-related utility failures, your emergency kit is your lifeline.

Remember your emergency steps:

- Have your Survival Kit
- Ensure your family's plan has been practiced and communicated to everyone
- Continually monitor National Weather Services, NOAA, and other media outlets for alerts
- Know your best shelter options at home or on evacuation routes
- Shut off utilities to prevent secondary events such as gas leaks and fires from downed power lines

Surviving Outdoors: You Need Basic Grab Bags

A survival kit is not something that only conspiracy nuts should have! The idea of a survival kit usually conjures images of someone waiting for the world to end. A kit is essential to caring for and protecting your family from occurrences at any time and place.

A basic kit could more aptly be called a safety kit or a sustainment kit; it will help protect you during emergencies, from severe storms to stressful situations. Some people refer to a kit as a "to go" kit, but I use the term a "grab bag" because your kit should be…stocked and ready to grab!

Before you run out and buy supplies to make your kits or purchase ready-made kits, remember that the best kit won't substitute for planning. An easy way to remember the concept is to keep your HEAD…handy essential assets, which means you can deal with the situation and not panic!

H – *Have* your kits *handy* and tell people where you are staying or going.

E –*Essentials* are a priority, and while they might include your kits, your first step is to ensure that you are appropriately dressed and ready to react. Wearing too many clothes is better than running into the event in your sleepwear or for a day at the beach.

A -*Assets* needed to survive include your Grab Bag kits, but you also need to consider your surroundings, the weather, and the available resources.

D - *Deal* with the situation, *don't panic* when an emergency occurs. Being calm will be one of your greatest assets in a crisis.

Knowing shelter, keeping warm, and administering first aid are critical requirements. Get those issues resolved, and you have plenty of time to deal with water and food issues.   Remember that hypothermia can kill you in minutes, unlike thirst and hunger, that first use your body's natural storage for days.

Ready-made bags can be purchased from stores such as REI for less than $200. You can make your own for much less, and they will be specific to what you and your family require.

Grab Bags Survival or Safety Kit

Now that you've decided you can keep your head, it is time to address the basic kit's core components. These kits initially prepare you for being away from home or needing to leave home in an emergency. We've already looked at what to store for an At-Home situation, and hopefully, you could take those supplies. You should have a separate Grab Bag for a quick dash if not.

To meet your emerging priorities outside the home, you need— Shelter, Fire, Signals, Water/Food, and First Aid. Once these four core packages are squared away, kits for the nice-to-have items can be addressed.

The core kit includes the following:

Shelter Kit:

- 2 or 3 reflective silver emergency blankets (mylar)
- 1 Poncho or tarp
- 1 piece, minimum 6' x 6' sheet of 3 mil plastic
- 1 coil of 50' parachute cord
- 1 roll of duct tape (any cold-resistant tape works)
- Knife

Life's Sustainment Rule

- Survive only three minutes without air
- Survive in extreme cold for three hours without shelter
- Survive three days without water
- Sustainment is possible without food for three weeks

A Paracord Bracelet- an easy way to carry an emergency cord; wearing a couple of these gives you the cord you need. They are sold almost everywhere, or you can make your own.

The emergency blankets can serve as a shelter and a heat reflector in a dire situation. The blankets should have a sturdier material as a backing to help strengthen their ability to provide cover.   The 3mil sheeting can provide added durability. Cutting a cord long enough to tie between two trees at about three feet from the ground will support the blanket lean-to or pup tent, just like you used to make as a kid.

Use the tape to secure one edge of the blanket and plastic to the cord, and find branches, rocks, dirt, or snow to secure the back edge to the ground. Use the other blanket on the floor of your shelter and add pine boughs, leaves, or anything else you see that will help insulate and add comfort for you. A poncho can often double as your plastic, your floor, or your roof. A poncho is not just for keeping the rain off of you.

I've made a game of doing this with grandkids as a fun activity; who says you must be a Boy Scout. Remember, having a child's imagination and an adult's skills can prepare you for all sorts of out-of-the-box thinking…nothing is impossible.

Fire Kit:

Add a fire kit to the shelter kit, depending on why you are not safe at home; you can use this kit for warmth, cooking, or signaling.

- 2 each, containers of matches (strike anywhere stick type), in waterproof containers
- Disposable lighter
- 1 fire-starting tool
- 2 each, steel wool, #0000, in sealed bags, a separate 9V battery
- 2 candles (slow-burning emergency candles are good)

The matches, fire-starting tools, and a candle make sense, but why the steel wool? Steel wool is a lightweight and easily flammable material with just a spark from a flint or a battery. You will have a fire if you have a nine-volt battery and touch both terminals to the steel wool.

A candle will provide light, but most importantly, you can use the melted wax to make "fire starters" by rubbing the wax into a piece of cloth, and you can dip your matches in the wax to make them waterproof.

Signal Package:

If you are stranded by weather and want to be found, being able to signal for help can be lifesaving, particularly if you don't have enough supplies to last a while.

- 1 glass 'G.I.'-type signal mirror
- 1 whistle, plastic 'coaches' type
- 1 fluorescent orange cloth signal flag, 3 foot by 3 foot

The orange cloth and a signal mirror will help attract attention, as will your silver reflective shelter blankets. A signal mirror works with a more directed reflection than a regular mirror. The whistle will allow you to "call" for help much longer and louder than shouting.

Water and Food:

We know water is critical if you are out for more than a day or so. Food and water will sustain you and help you think more clearly if you want to be found. If you don't want to be seen, you hopefully took your more significant At Home food cache.

- 6 gallons of water per week/per person
- Water purification tablets
- Pot or container for water purification
- Food staples —easy to carry, store, and high energy

Water and food should be stored in airtight food grade plastic cans or glass containers. When at home or in a freezer location, store your water in the freezer; if power is lost, the frozen water will help keep other foods frozen until the water is needed and thawed. Water purification is required when fresh, clean water is unavailable; otherwise, to prevent illness. Not a problem if you can grab your stored water from home

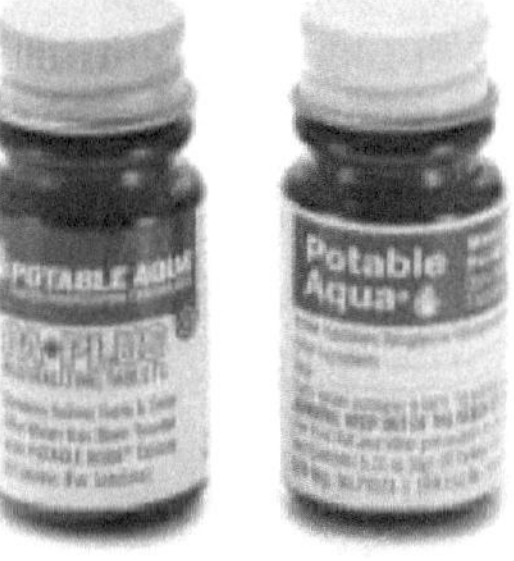

before leaving. You should be fine if your kit contains purification tablets or chlorine bleach.

Food items should only be items that you enjoy eating. Still, good choices include peanuts, crackers, dry cereal, canned, bottled, or boxed juices, canned vegetables, canned entrees, dried fruits, non-perishable cheeses, dried meat, powdered milk, canned meats, peanut butter, and meat spreads. Be sure to rotate pantry supplies to ensure that your emergency provisions remain viable and fresh.

Your pantry stock can assume that you are at home when an emergency strikes but plan on what you would take if you needed to evacuate your home; it is even more important that your food is compact, lightweight, and can be consumed without cooking.

First Aid:
- First Aid Book (don't count on Google helping you)
- Basic Kit
- Personal Medications

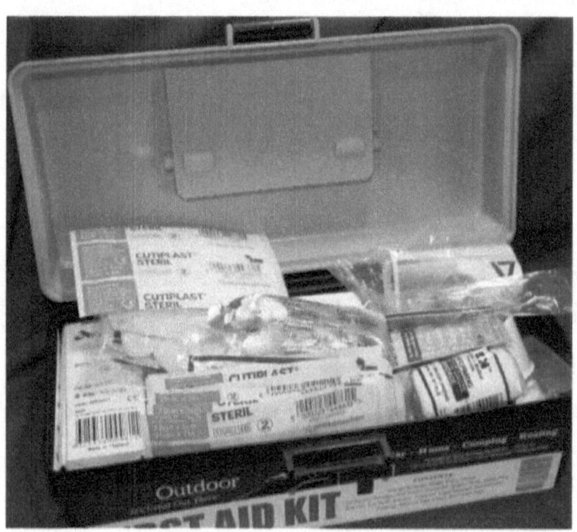

These five core kits: shelter, fire, signals, food/water, and first aid, will serve the most basic needs for the short-term situation. The shelter, fire, and signal items should be packed in one backpack or container. Water and food provisions should be ready to go but kept in a separate carry-all in a cool, dry storage area. A first aid kit is vital regardless of survival planning; this kit can be kept handy for family outings.

An emergency tool kit is also a great addition to have handy and ready to go. Making the first aid kit and the tool kit has many variables and isn't as basic as the core five. We will address each type of kit: shelter, fire, signal, water/food, tools, and first aid kit in more detail.

Don't Panic; keeping your head is critical. The first instinct is a shock when forced out of your home, which can be paralyzing. You must push yourself through this and adapt to your plan of action. Let your adrenaline move you forward to enact your emergency plan. You are prepared; no need for panic because you can handle anything. Be Observant…Be Confident…Be Creative; you can survive.

"It's better to be prepared for an event and not have one than to have an opportunity to use your grab bag and not be prepared.

Shelter Bag

Emergencies don't just happen when you are comfy and secure inside your home with the power and water working. In many cases, you should plan on the potential of having to leave your home or being stranded outside. A quote by Karma Metzgar, a nutrition specialist at the University of Missouri Extension, sums it up, "don't expect that the tap will flow and the lights will glow."

Having a shelter is the priority of survival. If you can protect yourself and your family from outside elements, heat, cold, and wind, the chances of surviving or being rescued in an

emergency are significantly increased. When adequate protection is established, you can deal with less heat, last for three days without water, and more than three weeks without food!

Wearable Shelter

If you plan to leave your home, the first thing you can do is get dressed appropriately. In the prior section, we mentioned a shelter grab bag, but the clothing you wear is even more primary than the shelter bag. This is a mistake! Clothing is the first line of shelter, and in all, your planning with family is often overlooked.

Some families practice fire drills with their families; they have a route out of the house and a spot to meet. This drill also works for any emergency. Knowing that situations and emergencies can happen at any time of day or night, when you are home and when you are not, is a step in your planning.

Being adequately dressed is a must! Watching news programs shows us people being forced out of their homes in pajamas or fleeing from other disasters with only the clothes on their backs...sometimes those clothes aren't very practical.

There is a big difference between what you might wear to make a fashion statement and what you will wear to be comfortable and able to take a long walk. Thinking of clothing in terms of, "If I am required to walk home, how should I be dressed," make clothing choices more transparent. Depending on the season or location you live, make sure that any emergency plans include having these "walking" clothes available for emergency use.

In-home drills have a bag for you and your children to grab with your emergency ladder or stashed in a garage or area that gives you quick and easy access. It is not over-planning or paranoia; it is thoughtful planning.

When you have time to prepare for evacuation due to weather or other sudden events, be sure you are dressed to provide your body protection from the sun, wind, and cold. Wearing several layers of light clothing is better than one or two heavy garments. Layering allows you to adjust to varying conditions and can help avoid both hypothermia and heatstroke.

When you remember that clothing is the shelter you wear on your body, and your emergency plan includes the garments and items you need, you are well on your way to being prepared. Being dressed for the weather items can consist of the following, but adjust for your season:

- Dress in layers -Shirts, sweaters, jackets, or coats- removing or adding layers as you become too hot or too cold can be a lifesaver.
  Pants in layers are also helpful unless you live in a climate that has a steady temperature; you may want shorts during the day and long pants at night. Know your area and clothing needs.
- Hat or caps – I'm sure you hear your mother's voice telling you not to go outside without your hat…Listen!
    - Water repellent and warm are operative words for cold-weather gear. Winter caps can keep almost fifty percent of your body heat from escaping…this is true no matter how thick-headed you or others may think you are. Ski caps and snow masks are convenient.
    - A vented cap or sun hat will help prevent sunstroke by protecting and giving shade while allowing heat to escape.
- Gloves or mittens – Gloves are fantastic in any weather because you can use them to protect your hands from possible cuts and scrapes while trying to survive outdoors. Mittens are best for cold weather because they trap the heat of your hand and let all your fingers share in their mutually generated heat. But mittens make it hard to do some tasks. A pair of thinner garden-style gloves under mittens is a good option for many people and situations.

o   Footwear – it may be summer, but don't run out of the house with just any shoes. Make sure you have shoes covering your entire foot; no clogs, crocs, sandals, flip flops, or open-toed shoes. You may only be out of the house for hours, or depending on the reason you are leaving may be away from home for an extended period. Shoes protect your feet from the elements and injury. All-terrain type or athletic shoes are the right choice. Boots with felt liners are suitable for damp or cold; regardless of the footwear, be sure

you are also wearing socks. Blisters and infections of the feet can bring you to your knees, literally!

Once you are sure that you are dressed for emergencies, you are ready to take on the task of having a temporary shelter bag prepared. The shelter kit will serve many purposes, providing a sheltered place to rest or sleep and offering rain, snow, and wind protection.

In reviewing your bag, it needs to include Mylar emergency blankets, either a poncho, tarp, or plastic sheeting, which can all be used as rain gear when you are on the move. The dual-purpose items are the best way to travel while giving you maximum protection lightly.

External Shelter

If an event is severe enough to force you out of your house and away from urban environments, then you probably expect this to be a longer-term event. When longer-term evacuation from your home is required, choose a shelter site that offers windbreaks, is close to a water source, a clearing large enough to allow signaling, and is free of other foreseeable perils.

The need for shelter is critical and secondary to only one thing...the need to breathe. So, choose an area wisely. Avoid sites that would not be susceptible to rock slides, avalanches, flooding, or excessive wind. If you are trying to stay off the grid purposely, you can ignore the need for an open space that would provide an open area for signaling!

A sturdy rock outcropping creates a natural sheltering nook. When in snow, dig out around the base of a tree, using the tree branches to tie emergency blankets, tarps, or ponchos for a quick "home away from home." Digging a dugout in snow about a yard wide and six or seven feet long can provide shelter for one person. Make it big enough to be comfortable when lined with pine boughs but not large enough to reduce the insulation qualities of a snow hut.

Tip = Keep your body from direct contact with the ground and snow. It isn't about comfort but ensuring that you have twice as much insulation below you as above to keep in your body heat. Make an insulating bed using small sticks, twigs, pine boughs, leaves, etc.

In warmer weather, assuming you don't have a small, lightweight backpack tent in your car for easy access, use your shelter kit and imagination. Think about all the imaginative ways as a child you used to come up with to build "tents" and "forts." You had an entrance that could be closed, it was compact (sometimes because mom only let you get one or two sheets dirty!), and these tents could be draped and fastened anywhere.

Plan for the long term, pray for the short term

As we discussed in the previous chapter, your shelter kit can be used to create a simple shelter, but I don't think there is only one way we discussed to make your tent. Emergency blankets, tarps, ponchos, or whatever else you can find to make a lean-to tent can save your life. In an emergency, you need to have the imagination of a child with an "anything is possible" attitude.

Having a lightweight, inexpensive tent in your car or shelter bag isn't always possible, but if you can stash a tent for ready use, you

can be ahead of the plan. When you don't have a tent handy, think of easy and quick options, such as making a tube tent.

A tube can be made by gluing (with waterproof glue) or using waterproof duct tape to join the edges of a small tarp or plastic drop cloth to create a tube. Use the rope or line in your grab bag to run through each end of the tube. Tie the ends between two trees, and you have a quick, easy shelter.

Your first thought may be that you don't need shelter...you are appropriately dressed, and help will arrive shortly...reality is that proper planning and actions at the beginning of an emergency are never a wasted effort. A perfect lean-to or tent can be made by finding two trees that are close enough together to use your cord or a fallen limb to act as your roof ridgeline. Layering other limbs or your shelter materials can make a warm temporary lodge.

Making a sturdy shelter may be the difference between life and death for you or a party member. Take action first; then, you can think back later that you didn't need such a sturdy, cozy home.

Using nature to build a shelter

- o A lean-to can be made totally from limbs and leaves. Using upright trees or even fallen logs can be the support you need. Then leaning fallen limbs or branches from the ground to the 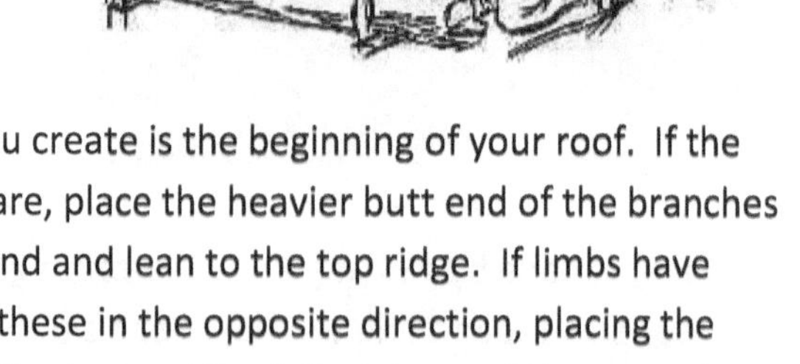 ridgeline you create is the beginning of your roof. If the limbs are bare, place the heavier butt end of the branches on the ground and lean to the top ridge. If limbs have leaves, put these in the opposite direction, placing the butt end at the top and the foliage toward the ground.
- o Roof ridgeline, then beams spaced evenly going from the ridge to the eave (in this case, the ground), and then boards crosswise to the beams. Laying limbs crosswise

across your other branches creates the basis of a roof. Think in terms of building a house roof...

- o   Finally, you are ready to roof your shelter, but instead of shingles, you will use what is available in your emergency kit. If you don't have anything available, it is not a problem. Look for fir trees, pine boughs, or other limbs with foliage to make a thatched roof.   People have lived in homes with thatched roofs for generations, and in some countries, they still use this type of roof.

Photos from NASA Spaceward Bound survival training

Remember, anything is possible; use your childlike imagination, adult skills, and experience! Your shelter should be the most secure and comfortable shelter that has ever been erected!

Fire Starting

The ability to start and maintain a fire is critical. Build a fire to provide heat, boil water, cook, provide light, the signal for help, and finally, deter wildlife.

Remember the motto; "always be prepared." as crucial as fire starting is to self-sustainment, it should not be packed and put away until needed. Practice using your gear before an emergency; your lives depend on your skill and knowledge. Doing this on a camping trip or in the backyard will be great fun for your children.

The basic uses that we need:

- o Heat protection – use fire to warm your body and dry your clothes

- o Signaling – search parties from both the air and ground can see an ever-burning fire

- o Lighting – having a light is a psychological impact, as well as a functional need for working when it becomes dark, and saves the battery life of other light sources

- o Purifying and sterilizing source – melted snow can provide water, and boiling water can protect against harmful bacteria

- o Cooking- hopefully, you have many items in your food kit, particularly if you took your survival buckets that don't need to be cooked. Save items that require cooking for one meal per day. If you didn't bring your larger food cache, try catching fish.

o   Protection – even primitive man realized that fire could offer protection and deter wild animals from coming into your camp, bringing back those protective instincts.

Fire Location

The fire pit site should be carefully selected, close to the tent for reflective heat, but not close enough to the shelter or covering trees. Maintaining a fire near your tent can provide directive heating to help with the cold. If your emergency occurs in a warm season or climate, adding more space between the shelter and the fire would be best.

While a fire is critical, it can also make you too warm and result in dehydration or sweat-soaked clothing; neither is a result you want.

Fire Ignition 101

Let's review the items that were in your Fire kit grab bag: containers of matches (strike anywhere stick type kitchen matches) in waterproof containers, a disposable lighter or two, one fire-starting tool of your choice (flint, metal matches, etc.), steel wool, 9V battery, #0000, in sealed bags and candles, all items suitable for fire starting. But nature also presents many things that you don't need to pack.

Look around at nature's bounty. When you know what to look for, you can find all sorts of items to use without depleting your kit prematurely.   But first, let's discuss preparing your fire site for the best results.

If the weather is dry and the ground is just waiting to start a forest fire, a little extra safety is required. Quickly ignited debris needs to be removed and gathered in your fire area. If you are in a location with rocks available, a ring of stones around the fire pit area will help prevent the unintentional spread of fire. This tinder will be great for starting a fire, but first, you need to get down to bare earth.

If the weather is rainy or snowy, then digging down to bare earth is still a good idea, and the wet ground around your fire pit will prevent the spread of fire. Starting your fire on a non-porous rock or green branches will be beneficial if the soil is wet. Once your area is cleared, you can identify your fire-starting sources or tinder.

Nature's tinder includes many burnable items- Small dry twigs,
dry leaves, moss, dead logs, dry pine needles, dried-out bark from fallen limbs, Cattails, dried animal dung, and dead grass.

To start your fire, have plenty of fire material available and store it in a dry place; your kit bag, lean-to, or under the umbrella of a tree. After gathering enough material, start with a small, loosely piled, broad base cone. If you have paper, bandages, cotton balls, wood shavings, and other easily flammable materials, these can be used too.

If the materials were dry, a match or your lit candle should be able to start the fire. When the fire sparks, it is essential to gently blow or fan the fire as you add slightly larger twigs about the size of your thumb before you bury the flames with larger logs.

Useful Hints

- o Don't waste matches by trying to start a poorly prepared or wet firebase
- o Make sure you build your fire before you need it; creating a fire after dark makes the task harder
- o Keep any paper, cardboard, or unneeded cloth. Remember, in the first chapter; we talked about the benefits of putting candle dripping on cloth for easy ignition

    o   Be creative; remember how you learned to start a fire from a magnifying glass, well the lens from binoculars will work, as will your signaling mirror

If you were prepared and had your fire kit packed, you had steel wool and a 9V battery. Touching the terminals to small tuffs of steel wool will quickly ignite. If you were well prepared and armed, you could also use gunpowder to help start a fire (never drop the entire shell into the fire).

Other items that you might have available could include using the seat material from your car. Assess your environment and looks at all the possibilities. Additional preplanning items that can be added to your fire grab bag include dryer vent lint, sawdust, or wood shavings; stored in a waterproof container is helpful.

Photo courtesy of Light My Fire Swedish fire starter

Once you have your little tinder fire going from whatever means you employed, it is time to add longer burning items to the fire. Limbs should be dried and not green wood. Don't worry about taking the time to saw or cut the limbs into perfect lengths; this takes too much energy and wastes time. Place whole logs across your fire pit, which will burn in the middle, and then the shorter remains can be pushed into the fire.

Protect your fire if rain looks imminent. Place limbs crosswise about a foot or so above the fire. As your fire continues to burn, the wet wood will eventually burn.

Dos and Don'ts Review:

- o Do not build a fire on top of grass that may catch fire and spread
- o Making a fire under a snow-covered tree could result in melting snow soaking into your shelter
- o Try and build a fire with a wall of rocks that will reflect heat toward your tent in cold weather
- o Your "camp" location is, hopefully, a location that provides nature's kindling. First, start the fire with available twigs (smallest to more substantial) and dry tinder such as leaves. If unsuccessful, then use your fire starter items in your grab bag.

As we mentioned earlier, an emergency is not the time to learn how to make a fire. Once you have selected your campsite and where your fire pit will be, it is time to get busy and make a fire. The caveman may have discovered fire accidentally, which took a while, but you are smarter and brought items you have the skill to use.

Signal Pack

While this pack won't keep you sheltered or warm, it is vital in summoning help. Hopefully, rescue or your ability to return to your home would be short-lived, but the reality is that some emergencies will last for weeks until rescue.

There are two goals here; first, to let someone know where you are, and second, to let someone know you need help. Being prepared and learning how to signal for help is critical. Knowing how to build a fire before you need a fire is also true for signaling.

You must have some signal gear in your emergency kit, but you can also find items around your shelter site to signal for help. The glass G.I. type signal mirror is the best type of ground-to-air signaling during sunlit hours.

 The signal mirror can be a standard-sized 2x3 business card size or a larger size. To use the signal mirror to reflect sunlight and signal, you hold the mirror up to your eye and look through the sighting hole. A bright spot will appear. When you hold the mirror close to your eye and turn it slowly, you can aim the spot at a target.

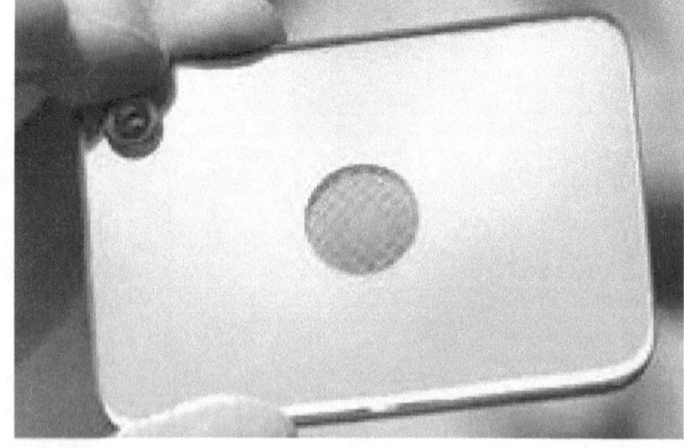

Photo from Coughlan's Mirrors

Moving the mirror will

create flashes to provide a signal. These mirror flashes can be seen miles away! In daylight, the mirror flash is possibly visible for 10 miles or more. The brightness of this mirror will generate 5 to 7 million candlepower of light.

During the night, using a flashlight or candle near the reflective surface provides a signal flash but is dependent upon the brightness of the light source. While a signaling mirror is suitable for long-range and uses light, noise is also necessary for signaling.

Keep a whistle in your grab bag kit. A plastic coach-style whistle will work, but since your ability to be found could depend upon

the whistle, it might be best to select a metal whistle.

The main decision in suitability is the user's comfort with the whistle. A metal whistle won't break in harsh conditions but is not the only choice when looking for a good survival item. Some whistles have built-in compasses and also serve as a waterproof match holder.

A fluorescent orange cloth signal flag, 3 feet by 3 feet, is also good for attracting attention. It can be waved or tied to offer a signal. Depending upon the season and your location, signaling is best done only during daylight hours. The flag can remain at any hour as an indication of the need for help.

We have all seen the cartoons of people stranded on a desert island writing HELP in the sand. But writing messages does work! While you can't carry items in your kit for other types of signals, you should be prepared to know and use international signals for help.

Unless you are trying to survive on a desert island, you must find a large enough clearing to leave messages. Writing out SOS or HELP can work, but make the words extremely big and, if possible, use your orange signal flag, clothes, and other items to create contrast and attention. Unfortunately, the clearing may be away from your campsite, and you must provide directions to your site.

Symbols developed for international civil aviation use the arrow to point to the location of your camp. Since the signal or sign must be large enough to be seen from the air, the standard should be three or more feet high and 30 feet long. Obviously, this will not be made of materials brought in your signal kit but can be made with natural items in your location.

Scooping away sand may take time, but it is possible, and as long as the signal is made far enough

away from the tide line, it won't need to be made multiple times. In snow, signaling is still possible by tamping out snow to attract attention.

Signals of this type can be made in sand and snow. But what about the most likely location of an open field? If the area is open and grass can be stomped down or cut down, it is possible to cut the signal into the grass. Use tree limbs, debris, rocks, or whatever you can scavenge to help make signals.

Standard Civil Symbols for rescue in addition to the arrow:

- o   V- Requires assistance
- o   X- Needs medical help
- o   N- means no
- o   Y- means yes

A long-held practice is also to use fire and smoke to signal for help. Signaling fires can make your "V" symbol for assistance visible. Creating three fire pits in a large triangle formation of thirty feet or more will work as a signal in sand, snow, or clearings.

Have only one fire burning until you hear aircraft above; having already built the fires but having lit the other two fires is essential. Once you hear potential help approaching light, the other fires. The flames will provide a triangle of fire which will alert planes to your need to help

Besides fire, the use of smoke is an important signal. The ability to create a strong smoke presence first relies on your three fires but also requires a stockpile of items, such as green vegetation, to place on your already burning fire to create smoke.

As we discussed in building fires in the previous section, dry tinder and wood are used on the base of the fire, and when you have a handy pile of green branches, leaves, and plant fauna to put on top of the fire, a lot of smoke will be produced. Bigger is better with these fires, but be careful to contain the fires.

Signal Fire Tips

- o Choose the smoke color that will be most visible for your surroundings...snow and sand make the fire black, or for vegetation areas, make the fire white
- o Black smoke is created by burning high oil content items such as your tires, oil, and some plastics
- o Check your fires daily and your burnable items to create smoke to ensure that you are ready

Other signaling tips to remember are that three of anything is the international standard for distress (three-gun shots, three fires, three flares, etc.) Reflection, from a mirror, a watch, or anything else that will reflect light, will work to provide a signal. Create a reflection that can be given in three bursts of light.

To be rescued, combine all these methods to make yourself as visible as possible.

Water

In today's world, we are used to having water on demand, available almost everywhere and anytime. Turn on a faucet, and grab a bottle of water from the store, gas station, or fast-food drive-through. But what if you are not near any places to get water due to an emergency? Then what do you do? Do you have an emergency plan or supply?

Your plan should include about 6 gallons of water per week/per person. Also, you should have purification tablets, a purification filter system, and a pot for boiling water if you are sheltering outside. Your water and supplies should be stored in a food-grade container and ready to go.

"You can't predict the future, but you can plan for it."

If you are away from home and in the wild, water can be used faster than usual in extreme situations. A healthy adult in an average climate and not in a difficult situation can survive well on a little less than a gallon per day or about 13 cups of water.

Acquiring Water

Since water is essential to survival, it is worthwhile to plan actions to support longer-term outages without resorting to rationing. Being away from home means the methods we discussed in the Stay Home section won't work when you are out in the woods. Having the means to purify non-potable water or use an alternate water source will help curb the inclination to ration.

Employ "water discipline," but use your body as natural storage instead of rationing water.

Water for more than a week becomes a large ration to store or carry and may be impractical, so having the plan to acquire water to sustain you during a prolonged event is essential. Water discipline is a planned daily requirement. It should not be a rationing plan that limits consumption, creating a voluntary dehydration scenario.

Here are some tips for acquiring water if you didn't prepare for being out in the rough:

- Do not assume that a stream or other water source that looks clean is okay to drink. Can you tell by the site that the water is free from bacteria? The risk is not worth drinking or cooking with untreated or filtered water. Use purification tablets or a filtering bottle before drinking.
- During rainstorms, collect as much water as possible in containers you might have.
- In cold climates, collect snow and ice, then place the containers someplace warmer than 32° to thaw the water.

Purifying Water

Purifying non-Potable water is essential before drinking. Using tablets or filters will help remove bacteria and chemical elements in the water. Having the knowledge and supplies in your Grab Bag for purifying and preparing water can mean the difference between a healthy experience and a tragedy.

There are numerous brands and types of purification products on the market and natural methods. Spend time becoming familiar with the choices and consider the easiest ways. However, be prepared to improvise if your supplies are lost or run out.

Regardless of the brand, a reliable purification and filtration system will be certified to remove harmful bacteria, protozoa, or cysts like E. coli, cholera, and Salmonella

Simple processes for purification

- Water Purification system – Many different types and brands of commercially available filtering systems exist. These devices work well but are only as effective as the user's level of experience and knowledge. Make sure you know how to operate it and, in the best case, have the instructions with the system.

- Tablets and Chemical Additives – Pre-packaged tablets are a small, easy resource for water purification. Several chemicals can be used to treat water if you run out of tablets. Chlorine dioxide will kill all organisms after about four hours of treatment. Iodine will also be helpful but won't address all contamination.

- Straining- Using multiple layers of fine mesh fabric for straining and introducing chlorine or other purifiers will suffice with many water sources. Straining water before using a commercial filter will also help preserve your water purification system and prevent clogging.

- Filtering- Making layers of sand, grass, and charcoal will provide purification. Create a funnel or cone to pour the water through the filtering material to fill a storage container.

- Boiling water – Boiling water will kill bacteria and other disease-causing microorganisms commonly found in waterways. Depending upon the area's elevation, the length of time for boiling and the temperature attained may need to be adjusted. For example, at sea level, water will not rise above 212 °F (100 °C) when boiling. This temperature will kill most bacteria but not all pathogens. If you were at home, you could use a pressure cooker to elevate the level to approximately 244 °F. Pouring boiled water back and forth between pots after boiling will remove the flat taste associated with boiling.

More Complex processes for purification

- Activated Charcoal- While boiling will eliminate most pathogens, activated charcoal is necessary to remove pollutants. Boiling water first, bringing the water to a rolling boil for one minute, and then using activated charcoal for filtering will address biological and chemical contaminants.

- Distilling- You may have purchased distilled water for use in machines, irons, or other items for which you did not want chemical water deposits. In a survival situation, you can also use distilling to purify water. Seawater can be distilled and filtered to remove the salt.

- Evaporation Still – This still will produce water continuously using four basic items: plastic sheeting, a container, a shovel, and tubing. By digging a hole with sloped sides and placing the container in the middle of the hole, "evaporated" water will be stored. The clear plastic sheeting will create a greenhouse effect with the condensation formed from plant material in the spot. Using the tube to run from the container to ground level will allow the drinking operation of the still. *Diagram from National Agricultural Library, USDA*

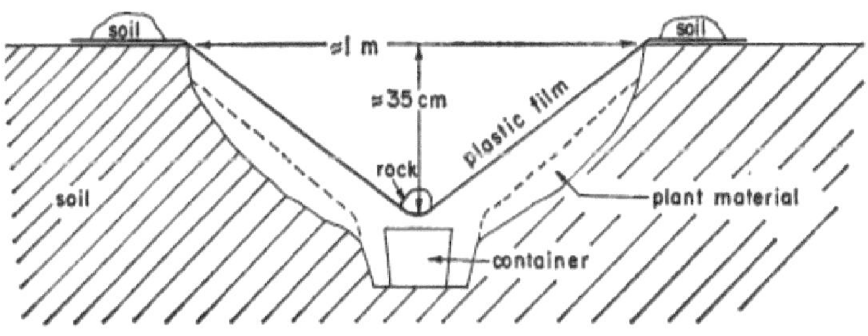

Regardless of how water is acquired or purified, we must have water to live. Having a stable and clean water source is one of the most basic yet essential skill sets necessary to sustain life in a survival situation. Avoid brackish water, don't drink urine, and be careful using salt water.

Finally, be sure to have a plan, be prepared, and utilize your knowledge to help you improvise, using some of the processes in this section.

Adding 16 drops of regular, non-scented household liquid bleach per gallon of water to make it safer to drink

Food

Your preparation for your food stores is invaluable for a Stay at Home event. When you must flee your home, grabbing those buckets could be the difference between going hungry or eating. Of course, your buckets were only intended to last for two weeks. If you want to stay away from civilization for any length of time, you will need to forage for food or make alternatives with anything you have remaining and what you can catch, trap or find.

There must be something serious going on around you if you are forced out of your house and stuck in the woods or other areas for an extended time. If this is the first time you have been out of an urban area, you probably don't have a lot of the skills necessary to be a hunter-gather. But there are things you can do to find sustainment.

When stores are not open, and foods can't be found, you can extend your chances of survival. As you already know, shelter and water are your most valuable resources, then food. You are likely to have some items remaining; now, find more to add to your supply.

If you are a hunter or take a rifle or gun with you, you may be able to track animals and shoot something to eat. Otherwise, you would need to trap or snare an animal. If that is the case, you need to look for paths, which are often to water sources because water is their top priority too.

You may be as picky as I am about what I eat, but anything that flies, hops, walks, swims, or crawls will be a possible food source. You also will need to look for edible plants. Types of traps are snares, traps, deadfalls, nets, or fishing lines.

Tips to remember:

• Don't eat umbrella-shaped flowers or mushrooms/fungi unless you are sure it is edible.

• Don't waste much energy catching an animal unless you will get more energy from the animal than it took to capture.

• Do eat any mammal or fish, but not their internal organs.

• Don't eat bulbs unless you are sure they are wild onions and garlic and not a look-a-like.

• Don't eat red (only 50% are edible) unless you know they are raspberries, and yellow or white (only 10% are edible) berries, as many are poisonous. Blue and blackberries are usually 90% safe.

• Do trust that most single-stem fruits on trees are safe, but they could cause stomach upset.

• Don't eat plants with milky sap or shiny leaves. The only exception would be dandelions.

• Don't eat any raw game or fish, and don't eat anything that appears sick or is acting strangely.

Finally, the most challenging choice I would have is eating insects, but they can sustain you. Avoid insects with bright colors, fuzzy ones, stinging or biting ones. Eat toasted worms and grubs, crickets, and grasshoppers (with wings and legs removed)

Fishing could be easily accomplished with items you had in your kits, dental floss, and safety pins if you didn't have a rod and reel. It's best to go fishing in the morning and at dusk. You can use your crickets, worms, and grasshoppers as bait. Fishing in lakes and rivers can provide Bass, Catfish, Blue Gill/Sunfish/Perch, and other local fish.

It would be nice if you had a rod and reel or even a makeshift hook and line, but if not, you can use a net from your sting or floss. You can spearfish using a pointed limb and your safety cord. Stand in the water and be very still, keeping the spear in the water; when the fish is less than a foot away, jab the spear!

One of the more straightforward methods I have seen work well is using a plastic bottle or milk jug to create a trap for baitfish such as minnow and a woven basket type for larger fish. The principle in both cases is the same. Place something the fish can eat in a closed end of the trap and create a funnel for the fish to go into, but they can become trapped when trying to leave, and you can pull the trap out and collect the fish.

Jug method – cut the top off and invert it in the cut end you just made. Secure it with string, wire, or vines that you find. Cut a flap in the top so you can reach in to retrieve the fish. You will need to place the flap against the ground, place something substantial on top, or even tie it into place. The fish will swim in the funnel end you made, and you then can bring the trap up.

Basket method – using long sticks and vines or saplings, you can make a decent representation of baskets that have been used for hundreds of years to catch fish. You can use sticks for the main supports of the basket, about seven of them, and you can use vines, saplings (remove the other bark for more flexibility), and weave. Instead of leaving the top of the basket open, you will still create a more funneled open end.

Photo by pasja1000 / Pixabay

Photo by MabelAmber/Pixabay

Fishing with a basket is a primitive method, and your basket will be primitively made. You will weave your smaller flexible items around your larger sticks. You are out in the wild, so no one expects the basket to be as neat as one made by an experienced maker but to be useable for catching dinner. Pine cones or a mess of twigs tied to the bottom can secure your bait.

As an adult, you can forage any number of things to eat. When you look at people that have been prisoners of war or lost for periods, they can be extraordinarily gaunt but alive as long as they have liquids. You might not like them and lose some weight, but this would not significantly impact most of us.

Babies and young children are the ones that need nourishment that you might not be able to provide from the wild. Make sure any provisions you need to have for emergency baby formula are retained for that use. This recipe will stay safe to drink for two days.

Emergency Baby Formula:
Ingredients:
1/3 cup plus 2 Tbsp. Instant Powdered Milk
OR 1/4 cup Powdered Milk

1 1/2 cups Boiled Water
1 Tbsp. Oil
2 tsp. Sugar
Instructions:
Mix Powdered milk and water together.
Blend thoroughly.
Add oil and sugar.

First Aid

Providing first aid under outdoor conditions where emergency help might be delayed or nonexistent is a matter of making do with basic kit elements. It is challenging to prepare for every situation, so having a grab bag kit filled with bandages, antiseptics, painkillers, and other emergency items is necessary.

A typical dilemma in the wild is how to best treat an injury and whether or not an injured person should be moved. A severe and life-threatening injury may require that a person is left in a marked shelter while another person seeks help. Hopefully, a serious injury that requires professional medical support can be averted, and the survival first aid kit will suffice for the typical type of issue.

Your first-aid bag should include a first-aid manual, necessary first-aid items, and personal medications. Specific first aid training for wilderness care and certification is available for people that frequently travel or live in rural and secluded areas. Consider the type of issues and advanced level of care that can be provided with training.

Basic Assessment Tips:

- **Breathing**: Check for any lack of oxygen intake, as this can result in death within a few minutes.

- **Bleeding**: Stop bleeding as quickly as possible to avoid tissue damage and death.

- **Breaks**: Check for broken bones and stabilize them to avoid further damage, particularly compound fractures.

Basic First Aid Items	Minimum Qty
First Aid guide	1
Protective Masks (each person)	3
Hand Sanitizer Gel Bottle	1
Sterile Saline or Bottled Water	1
Nitrile Gloves (pairs)	4
Roll 2" & 4" Gauze	1
3"x3" Sterile Gauze Pads	4
4"x4" Sterile Gauze Pads	4
Adhesive Bandages 1x 3, 3/4 x2	20
Butterfly Bandages	15
Adhesive Tape (roll)	1
Alcohol Pads	30
Cotton Balls (sm. Bag)	1
Antibiotic Ointment	1
Antiseptic Solution	1
Sting/Burn/Sunburn/lip balm (ea.)	1
Antacid Tablets(roll)	1
Digital Thermometer	1

Aspirin (Packs)	10
Non-aspirin Tablets packs	10
Burn Cream (tube)	1
Cotton Tip Applicators	20
Finger Splint	1
Instant Hot & Cold Packs	1 ea.
Medical Scissors	1
Metal Tweezers	1
Penknife	1
Flashlight (and spare batteries)	1
Safety Pins	10
Waste Bag	1

In addition to the essential items, a more fully stocked kit could include the following:

- Snakebite kit,
- Magnifying glass,
- Anti-diarrheal medicine
- Tourniquet
- Un-waxed dental floss and needle for emergency stitches,
- Insect repellent
- Clove Oil
- Liquid Bandage or Super Glue in an emergency
- Hydrogen Peroxide
- Apple Cider Vinegar
- Dropper

Packing these items and any other products you normally use for support, such as allergy medications, non-latex products, and prescription medicines, could save your life. Be prepared, but don't make your kit so large and heavy that carrying it is impractical.

Why Peroxide?

- Treat cuts and scrapes to clean them.
- Mix 50/50 with water to treat foot fungus, and apply every night.
- A 50/50 mixture can be used for mouthwash and to treat canker sores, and when mixed with baking soda can be used to brush your teeth. Do not swallow.
- Help with yeast infections by mixing a tablespoon with warm distilled water for a douche.
- It can work like bleach to kill germs and mold and, when used with vinegar, be effective against bacteria.

Why Apple Cider Vinegar?

- Swimmer's ear is the first reason I have vinegar in my aid kit.
- Before packaged douches became available, vinegar and water were used to clean and help with yeast.
- Help Sunburn and insect bites/stings by applying cider to the skin
- Bruises can be improved by using a cotton ball soaked in vinegar and held against the injured spot for an hour.
- Help scalp issues and hair by using after shampooing.
- The spray of skunks can be helped with vinegar. Clothes can be soaked overnight.

Treatment for Unexpected Emergencies

A first aid manual would be handy to have in your Grab Bag. It is not medical advice, just common sense as a start to your knowledge base. The below items are the types of emergencies that you should avoid.

Animal Bites - Most animal bites are likely to become infected. Be sure to wash and disinfect the wound in the best possible way. Apply antibiotics and loosely bandage. Look for rabies in the animal, and check the wound frequently for signs of infection. Medical help should be pursued.

Cramps- Lack of water or salt and insufficient oxygen to your muscles are reasons for cramping. The best option is to avoid overdoing activities, keep hydrated, and, if exerting yourself, make sure you are breathing deeply. Immediately increase your intake of water and salt. Eating or drinking vinegar or mustard is a trick often used to help relieve the cramping. Do not pound your muscles to stop the cramps, which will add to soreness.

Ear Aches – A common issue for children, but ear aches from swimmer's ear can happen to anyone. An old but effective treatment when you can't go to the doctor is to use Apple Cider Vinegar dripped in the ear to clear bacteria.

Fractures- Stabilize broken bones with tape and use any material available to make splints. You do not want the broken bones rubbing together or poking through the skin. If the skin is broken, the break is more severe and should be seen by a professional immediately. In the meantime, you would treat this as a wound to stop bleeding and try to limit the chance of infection.

A broken arm can be taped to your body; broken ribs should be wrapped with tape to keep ribs from moving and ease breathing. Immobilizing the break is most important.

Insect/Spider Bites -Most insects and spiders you will run into will not create much more than an itchy spot. Bee stings for those that do not have a known allergic reaction may swell and hurt. Chiggers, fleas, mosquitos, and ticks are the most common biters you will run into, and they can cause more serious issues. Mosquitoes can be carriers of other diseases, such as the West Nile virus. Ticks can carry Lyme disease; they should be removed immediately by twisting them counterclockwise and pulling. Over the Counter (OTC) remedies can help with itching, such as Calamine lotion, Corticosteroids, and Antihistamines such as Benadryl or generic brands.

Avoid the black widow spider and some scorpions, as you will require medical attention.   Antivenins are available for these but won't be found in your First aid kit.

Snake Bites – Many snakebites are by non-venomous snakes and should be treated like an animal bite and rarely result in death. It is the venomous snakes that deserve your concern. If the area of the bite begins to swell and change color, the snake is most likely venomous, and you need immediate help. Coral, Copperhead, Cottonmouth/Water Moccasin, and Rattlesnakes are the most dangerous snakes.

Toothache- A toothache isn't life-threatening, but it sure can hurt. Applying clove oil to the tooth and gum area will help; taking pain relievers will also help. Avoid hot or cold on the tooth.

Wounds- Large wounds require medical treatment; you can offer immediate necessary help but need to seek proper attention. You can apply pressure with your hand and pressure bandages with spurting wounds.

Minor cuts should be cleaned and rinsed; an antibiotic should be applied before bandaging. Hydrogen Peroxide is suitable for cleaning but do not soak the skin for an extended time. Dressings should be changed, and if signs of infection become present, attention should be given by medical personnel.

Regardless of the severity of the wound, proper cleaning and disinfection are essential for more extended stays in the wilderness where evacuation is not deemed necessary or impossible. Relatively harmless local infections at the wound site can quickly escalate into life-threatening systemic infections if proper care is not taken. Some courses provide instruction on the appropriate administering of antibiotic drugs to help treat serious infections.

CPR (Cardio-Pulmonary Resuscitation) -CPR is helpful to know; however, the reality is that the patient is unlikely to survive without nearby medical facilities and care.

Hopefully, we won't ever need to live off the grid due to a natural or man-made event, but our preparation can save lives and protect families in most situations. Ready.gov offers an online course that prepares you to help until rescuers arrive.

Man-Made Hazards

Natural weather events aren't the only hazards that require you to react with your emergency kit. At the same time, we can wrap our minds around natural events such as earthquakes, landslides, tornadoes, hurricanes, and other weather events, but we don't expect to face the perversion of our fellow man. What a beautiful world it would be if we could trust humans to treat each other with peace and love!

This book isn't intended as a warning or an apocalyptic guide. Since the time of Cain and Abel, history has shown that wars and the destruction of our fellow man happen. Survival from a man-made or natural disaster other than chemical or nuclear events can be withstood with preparation. To think that we are safe and will never see a drastic devastation event is a nice thought. But is it realistic?

Chemical spills, nuclear accidents, widespread power interruptions, terrorist attacks, economic failures, pandemics, and other potential disasters can present serious hazards and peril to you and your family. None of us want to believe that any technological or biological hazards can occur accidentally, let alone as a planned attack.

During the "Cold War" from the 1950s through the 1980s, America was worried about the Communist Soviet Union dropping an Atomic bomb as each country struggled for dominance. For those old enough to remember the "Cold War" mentality of fallout shelters, bunkers, and nuclear drills taught in school, we now know how ridiculously naïve we were.

Extinction is the rule, survival is the exception. Carl Sagan

Since America dropped the A-bomb on Japan in World War II to end the war, you would think we knew enough to know that going to a shelter or getting under our school desks and covering our heads with our arms would not save us. Everyone was warned to know where their closest shelter was, usually in the basements of large buildings. Of course, some people built their underground or basement shelter and stocked for an extended stay.

Prepping your home for a terrorist or biological attack isn't something the average person is prepared to do. Our homes are meant to shelter us, not protect us from biological or chemical impacts. A unique ventilation system and safe room area would be required to survive this circumstance.

Photo by lenzius/Pixabay

The end of the "Cold War" mentality ending in the 1980s, during President Reagan's term, lulled Americans into thinking the "Evil Empire" was finished. After all, the United States hadn't been attacked on the North American continent since the early struggle for independence and the Mexican American War. Both countries had weapons of mass destruction, missiles, and rockets to thwart attacks, so we returned to thinking America was safe from attacks. Japan's attack on the territory of Hawaii at Pearl Harbor in 1941 was the last time the American people feared something like this.

However, twenty years after the Evil Empire was no longer a threat, the "Axis of Evil" emerged during President Bush's presidency, not as a specific foreign government-sponsored attack but as orchestrated terrorist group strikes. We sat glued to the television as images of planes flying into the World Trade Center in New York and the Pentagon in Washington DC instilled fear in everyone. There would have been more plane attacks, except for the brave passengers on another plane that took on the terrorist and crashed the plane well short of its DC target. Almost 3,000 people were killed, and more than 6,000 were injured in these attacks. For many Americans, our feeling of security and isolation from the attack ended that day.

TEOTWAWKI

The End Of The World As We Know It

www.prepperjournal.com

Nuclear Attacks and Accidents

Nuclear attacks seem unlikely with today's tit-for-tat arms deals and treaties. However, some countries do threaten and intimidate with random testing. It is still disheartening to know that there are at least 230,000 active nuclear arms worldwide, and human error or deliberate use could happen. We expect our government to present counter-attacks to prevent fallout over the US.

Nuclear accidents have happened and can happen at any nuclear site. In the US, fallout from the Three Mile Island accident impacted and displaced families. Initially, more than 140,000 people left their homes. Forty years after the event, there are still concerns about increased cancer rates among residents, even though the emissions were much less than what an attack would provide.

According to FEMA, sheltering in place may be necessary for approximately a month after an attack or accident. About 80% of fallout happens in the first 24 hours. The preparations of your Stay at Home food kits would be beneficial if you stayed or had to leave the area, you would at least have some necessities. Even if you were not in an area directly impacted, you could see shortages and issues with supplies unless you have a cache of goods to tide you over until normality can return.

There are 430 reactors worldwide, but oversight and monitoring reduce the risk of accidents. Unless a terrorist group caused an issue, we could feel pretty safe.

The best space to be in during an attack or accident puts as many solid walls, concrete, brick, and soil between you and the radioactive material.

Hazards related to nuclear explosions (www.ready.gov)

- **Bright FLASH can cause temporary blindness for less than a minute.**
- **BLAST WAVE can cause death, injury, and damage to structures several miles from the blast.**
- **RADIATION can damage cells of the body. Significant exposures can cause radiation sickness.**
- **FIRE AND HEAT can cause death, burn injuries, and damage to structures several miles out.**
- **ELECTROMAGNETIC PULSE (EMP) can damage electrical power equipment and electronics several miles from the detonation and cause temporary disruptions further out.**
- **FALLOUT is radioactive, visible dirt and debris raining down from several miles up that can cause sickness to those who are outside.**

Terrorism

Terrorist attacks on Americans overseas and in embassies abroad have always been a concern, but incidents on US soil were unexpected. There have now been numerous attacks of escalating violence on American Embassies and Americans overseas, but only in the past twenty years have we seen increasing violence on American soil.

Terrorists have used explosive devices as their most common choice of weapon around the world. In some areas, they coordinated attacks, wiping out whole areas with stolen and black-market arms. While you are unlikely to be a direct target of a terrorist bombing, you could be in the wrong place when an attack happens.

Domestic Terrorism- Defined as committing terrorist acts in the perpetrator's own country against their fellow citizens.

The idea of terrorist bombing or attacks is probably the most heinous of any event you could imagine or expect to encounter. Hopefully, your survival kit will never be needed to provide you and your family a means of avoiding this type of event. A scenario with a higher probability of occurrence is that you are temporarily impacted due to the residual impacts. The impact could include interruption of communication systems, dislocation from your home due to emergency response, fire/smoke, and the need to find your family member and arrange for alternate shelter.

However, if you should find yourself in the middle of a bombing or attack, utilize some common-sense approaches that apply in other situations where damages have occurred to a building.

- Protect yourself by finding cover from falling objects under a desk or table is an option, away from glass doors and windows. Once you believe it safe to evacuate, use the stairs, not elevators.
- Where there is smoke, there is usually fire, so touch doors before opening them, keep as low to the floor as possible to avoid smoke, and exit quickly.
- Once you are outside, enact your family emergency plan, which should include a check-in location for your family near work, school, or home, whichever is the closest point.
- If you should become trapped and have a flashlight or whistle, use them to signal for help when trapped, or

bang on pipes, walls, etc., to let rescuers know where you
are.

Even the diehard survivalist knows it isn't practical to have an
emergency kit with you at all times, but what is useful is keeping
your wits. Think about natural disasters such as fires and storms,
and remember your primary needs and responses. Knowing that
your family has a communication plan and a "readiness" mentally
will significantly enhance your focus and response to an event.

Mob violence is easily created, and agitation continues from
outside influences that could impact where you live. There are
many more incidents of what could be defined as domestic
terrorism, protests, and shooting that have the potential to drive
you from your home. In these events, you are likely to be able to
stay with family or friends if your home is affected.

In recent years we have seen
foreign impacts and influences
applied to political issues,
campaigns, funding of protests,
and more to impact America.
Attacks can be made against
almost every part of society and
be very covert.

Photo by
Bruce Emmerling/Pixabay

Recent political/social unrest had protestors take over an entire
area of Seattle. The place was taken over and called CHOP (The
Capitol Hill Occupied Protest) or CHAZ (Capitol Hill Autonomous
Zone), an area that protestors took over. Residents are now suing

the city, charging that the local Mayor supported the protestors and put businesses and residents at risk. What would you do, stay, or leave?

We can't always depend on the government to make the right choices for us. You need to be ready and able to take care of yourself. If there was a significant enough event, you might need to leave your home and find an area that is not an urban target. Political and social unrest is not a new idea, and all over the world, people have been affected by the disorder. There is nothing to prevent this from happening in your backyard.

"...there is no single, universally accepted definition of terrorism," but the U.S. federal code defines it as "the unlawful use of force and violence against persons or property to intimidate or coerce a government, the civilian population, or any segment thereof, in furtherance of political or social objectives." Washington Post, Brad Plumer, April 16, 2013

The end of your world, as you know it, could be a domestic event, nuclear or biological attack, or even a pandemic. As with all hazards, weather or man-made, you should be prepared to react, but don't panic. Be observant but not paranoid; seeing danger around every corner is a waste of energy and no way to live your life. Surviving an event would forever change the way you look at the world.

Biological Events

Nature's storms are easier to prepare for than man-made or biological events. Widespread biological attacks are less likely to

happen than a terrorist impact. Attacks on your safety don't need to be in the form of bombs. Bio-terror threats can be an intentional dispersal or release of an agent or poison to cause illness or death. Using bacteria, viruses, and toxins can be a weapon that is hard to defend against, is largely unseen, and creates widespread disruption.

Airborne toxins, as evidenced by the infamous Anthrax letter scare, show how difficult it can be to track and defend against a biological event. The U.S. Postal Service was the implement of delivery in this case. The cause of the attack may never be fully understood as the prime investigation target died before he could be arrested.

What is important to realize is the relative ease of hatching this plot and the randomness that killed five Americans, with seventeen more people becoming seriously ill from anthrax-laced letters in 2001. It is difficult to defend against the dispersal of toxins, particularly airborne biological hazards.

Prepare for the unknown by studying how others in the past have coped with the unforeseeable and the unpredictable. Genl. George S. Patton

In 2013 a Texas woman was charged with sending Ricin-laced letters to President Obama and the Mayor of New York City over gun rights. Had someone targeted you, it is possible that you would not know that your mail contained a toxic letter. In the case of Ricin, the poison can cause death within 36 hours.

Several methods are used for spreading the biological element depending on the source. Aerosols released into the air as a fine spray can spread for miles, infecting anyone inhaling the laced air. The spread of viruses by insects and animals is another dispersal method. Introducing toxins or other biological to the water and food supplies are apparent concerns.

Your sustainment kit won't necessarily contain items to protect you from a toxin attack. Still, if a biological event occurs in your area, you would be ready to hit the road and seek a safer area.

"a biological attack is the intentional release of a pathogen (disease-causing agent) or biotoxin (poisonous substance produced by a living organism)." Center for Disease Control

Your water and food can be boiled and cooked to kill most bacteria. A HEPA filter or multiple layers of cloth may help screen out but not eliminate all airborne pathogens. Each family member should know a meeting place if separated during a biological attack. As with other events, the best planning is to have communication plans ready.

Online support is available on Bioterrorism:
https://emergency.cdc.gov/bioterrorism

Pandemic from an innocent virus or as a Biologic Weapon

When the COVID-19 virus first appeared in China and information about this leak from a Lab surfaced, so did the rumors that China let a biological weapon lose. There have been many back-and-forth theories on how this virus started. It was easier to track how the virus traveled into the US and around the globe by tourists returning home.

COVID-19 appeared to be an accidental event and not an intentional attack. Regardless, it has created tremendous impact and economic pressures worldwide. The effect on business has lasted more than six months, and the end is not in sight. Schools closed, and planning for a new school year has many areas planning on remote homeschooling at the start of the 2020 – 2021 school year.

Work is being done to develop a vaccine by December 2020, but so far, no luck. Most people wear face masks; others believe it is their right to refuse or don't think the virus is any worse than the flu or a cold, but it is a political gambit to impact presidential elections.

As the beginning of the book pointed out, COVID-19 required home isolation, and severe impacts on food and other supplies remain. This time it didn't appear that the pandemic was a global biological agent spread on purpose, yet it shows how easily this could be done and the ruin it can bring. Being prepared with your own supplies wouldn't be overreacting.

Prevent the spread of germs by avoiding people...not just those who appear sick, but others who could be ill without knowing. Do not expose others if you are sick.

- o Cover your mouth and nose with a tissue before coughing or sneezing. Face Masks are suggested when around others.
- o Wash your hands often with soap and water to help protect you from germs and spreading germs to others. Use hand sanitizer when soap and water are not available.
- o Healthy lifestyle habits such as drinking plenty of fluids, sufficient rest, managing stress, and proper nutrition can make a difference.

It is easier to prepare and prevent, than to repair and repent. Ezra Taft Benson

The CDC lists Biological threats by categories, from the highest threat to the lowest:

Category A

Definition

- easily disseminated or transmitted from person to person;
- high mortality rates, the potential for major health impact;
- might cause public panic and social disruption

Agents/Diseases

- Anthrax (*Bacillus anthracis*)
- Botulism (*Clostridium botulinum* toxin)
- Plague (*Yersinia pestis*)
- Smallpox (variola major)
- Tularemia (*Francisella tularensis*)
- Viral hemorrhagic fevers, including
    - o Filoviruses (Ebola, Marburg)
    - o Arenaviruses (Lassa, Machupo)

Category B

Definition

- moderately easy to disseminate;
- result in moderate morbidity rates and low mortality rates;

Agents/Diseases

- Brucellosis (*Brucella* species)
- Epsilon toxin of *Clostridium perfringens*
- Food safety threats (*Salmonella* species, *Escherichia coli* O157:H7, *Shigella*)
- Glanders (*Burkholderia mallei*)
- Melioidosis (*Burkholderia pseudomallei*)
- Psittacosis (*Chlamydia psittaci*)
- Q fever (*Coxiella burnetii*)
- Ricin toxin from *Ricinus communis* (castor beans)
- Staphylococcal enterotoxin B
- Typhus fever (*Rickettsia prowazekii*)
- Viral encephalitis (alphaviruses, eastern equine encephalitis, Venezuelan and western equine encephalitis)
- Water safety threats (*Vibrio cholerae, Cryptosporidium parvum*)

Category C

Definition

- emerging pathogens with ease of availability; production, and dissemination;
- potential for high morbidity and mortality rates and major health impact.

Agents

- Emerging infectious diseases such as the Nipah virus and hantavirus

Source: National Center for Emerging and Zoonotic Infectious Diseases (NCEZID)

Fortune favors the prepared mind. Louis Pasteur

Chemicals and Hazardous Materials

There are different levels of chemical and hazardous items, ranging from accidents and deliberate use. The materials can create vapors, gases, aerosols, and liquids that can come about without any warning. Accidental spills or mixtures can happen in the house or be mixed by someone with ill intent. However, from the start, they can be deadly.

Once dispersed, some vapors or gases might have an odor, but many more will be odorless and tasteless.   Lethal chemicals can quickly result in nausea, loss of muscle function, respiratory distress, and burning sensations.

Many household chemicals are hazardous by themselves; however, when accidentally mixed can be lethal. I learned early in life not to mix bleach and ammonia, which put out a dangerous vapor and forced everyone out of the house. Most products will have a warning or caution about mixing with other items. It is best to use individually. The most dangerous products include oven, drain, toilet and bathroom cleaners, bleach, insect baits, insecticides, and fuels. While hazardous, these items are unlikely to be used in a deliberate attack.

Chemical spills are accidental and bad luck, but deliberate attacks require a plan and execution. Regardless, your family should have an idea of how to come together and where to meet, as you are likely to be spread between work, school, home, and other places.

When an attack is deliberate, several choices are deadly nerve agents. Sarin is one of the most dangerous and has been used as a chemical weapon by governments. Germany first used sarin in the 1930s. It was odorless and could be used to contaminate food, water, and air. The gas paralyzes the respiratory system and muscles, causing suffocation. According to the World Health Organization, "Sarin is 26 times more deadly than cyanide gas. Just a pinprick-sized droplet will kill a human."

Headline and article from the Washington Post, September 1st, 2013:

Sarin gas used in Syria attack, Kerry [Secretary of State] says

The Obama [US President] administration asserted Sunday for the first time that the Syrian government used the nerve gas sarin to kill more than 1,400 people in the world's gravest chemical weapons attack in 25 years as the White House intensified pressure on a skeptical Congress to authorize punitive military strikes against Damascus.

CDC Advises What to do if exposed?
- Sarin vapor is dense and settles to lower levels; make sure to get fresh air at higher levels. Go outside if indoors or high ground when outside.
- Remove clothing, never pulling clothes over your head, then immediately wash your entire body with soap and water before seeking medical attention. Sealed disposed of clothing in several plastic bags to stop further exposure. Rinse eyes with water for 10 minutes or longer if burning or blurry.
- Get medical attention and administration of Sarin antidote!

The CDC also advises that if you have notice of an attack and you are in your home, then you should do the following:

- Choose an internal room, on the highest level of your home, without windows, if you are in an area of chemical attacks
- You will need Duct tape, plastic sheeting, and scissors
- Cover all the openings, including vents, with the plastic and duct tape
- Having a room selected and pre-cut plastic would be most beneficial to have in your prep kit

Cyanides are another group that can be a lethal chemical weapon. It was first used in World War I and caused illness and death. In low amounts, this chemical can be harmless. An indication of the gas is a bitter almond odor, but it is not always present.

Inhaling Hydrogen Cyanide poses the highest risk and is how it can be used as a terrorist weapon. The body's cells are impacted in large enough doses, and the heart, respiratory, and nervous system will shut down.

Symptoms of exposures are:
- Weakness and confusion
- Headache
- Nausea/feeling sick to your stomach
- Gasping for air, labored breathing
- Loss of consciousness
- Seizures
- Cardiac arrest

Varying Toxicity of Chemical Agents

As the government chart shows, Sarin is the highest toxic chemical and takes the least concentration.   Other items on the list can be used with sufficient quantities.

The more toxic a chemical, the smaller the amount of chemical required to cause harm. The table compares the lethal concentrations in parts per million (ppm) for acute (all-at-once) exposures to some chemical weapons and some common industrial chemicals.

Chemical agent	Approx. lethal concentration* (in ppm)	
Some Chemical Weapons		
Sarin (GB)	36	
Hydrogen Cyanide**	120	
Some Industrial Chemicals		
Chlorine**	293	
Hydrogen chloride	3,000	
Carbon monoxide	4,000	
Ammonia	16,000	
Chloroform	20,000	
Vinyl chloride	100,000	

*Based on LC_{50} values in laboratory rats: exposure concentration for 60 minutes at which 50% of rats would die. Rats are used for toxicology tests in part because of similarity to humans, but they are likely to be more susceptible because they have higher metabolisms.

**Used both as chemical weapons and as industrial chemicals

Source: NRC, EPA, and ATSDR

Reporting by the Organization for the Prohibition of Chemical Weapons (OPCW), an entity set up in 1997 to help with chemical weapon disarmament and destruction, in 2019, there were a total of

72,304 metric tons of chemical agents and 97 production facilities.
Chemical weapons in wars have been banned; however, countries
have continued using them on their citizens.
Syria has a continuing record of using chemicals against its
countrymen in its continuing fight with rebels.

Control and tracking chemicals are crucial to keeping these from
being used by terrorists and governments against citizens.

**"A secure and resilient nation with the capabilities
required across the whole community to prevent,
protect against, mitigate, respond to, and recover
from the threats and hazards that pose the greatest
risk." FEMA**

It Makes Sense to be a Prepper

Maybe you've mentioned your interest in being a "prepper" or a "survivalist," and as your friends listened, you were met with silence. Worse yet, they tell you that you're crazy! In the event of a significant issue, those same friends might expect to share your supplies. Who's crazy now?

You are not Crazy, You are not Paranoid, You are not living in Fear! Not being prepared is crazy, if you ask me. At the very least, your family deserves the time and effort to be ready. If it is crazy to be prepared, why are so many government agencies established to track and advise when emergencies are in the making?

Don't Be Ashamed To Be a Prepper

Additionally, there is National Preparedness Month each September:

Week 1: Sept 1-5	Make A Plan
Week 2: Sept 6-12	Build A Kit
Week 3: Sept 13-19	Prepare for Disasters
Week 4: Sept 20-26	Teach Youth About Preparedness

The theme is: "Disasters Don't Wait. Make Your Plan Today."

Whether you are an Android or IOS user, numerous apps support alerting the public in cases of natural or manmade disasters. The Wireless Emergency Alert (WEA) sends cell phone notices of imminent dangers and AMBER alerts. WEA breaks down their signals into these groups:

- Imminent Threat Alerts that include extreme weather and other threatening emergencies in your area;
- Public Safety Alerts that are less severe than Imminent Threat Alerts;
- AMBER Alerts;
- Presidential Alerts during a national emergency
- Test Messages that are opt-in messages to support state and local WEA testing.

Photo by Ready.gov

The WEA notification is designed to get your attention with a unique sound and vibration repeated twice. These alerts will not break into your phone calls, except for a Presidential alert, but will alert you when you finish your call.   Check broadcasts and take action!

 Through its Ready Campaign, the Federal Emergency Management Agency (FEMA) educates and empowers Americans to take some simple steps to prepare for and respond to potential emergencies, including natural disasters and terrorist attacks.

Ready asks individuals to do three key things: get an emergency supply kit, make a family emergency plan, and be informed about the different types of emergencies that could occur and their appropriate responses.

All Americans should have some necessary supplies on hand to survive for at least three days if an emergency occurs. Individuals must review this list and consider where they live and the unique needs of their family to create an emergency supply kit that will meet these needs. Individuals should also consider having at least two emergency supply kits, one complete kit at home, and smaller portable kits in their workplace, vehicle, or other places they spend time. ***FEMA Publication www.ready.com***

I am amazed at the number of people I speak with that think being prepared seems like a waste of time and is paranoid. Being ready and prepared for any emergency is sane and safe!

A resource the government provides is FEMA's Prepareathon, which was created to motivate, communicate, and prepare individuals and communities to take action to protect themselves against disasters. Their stated goals are to help everyone understand:

- Disasters that could affect their community

- Know what to do to stay safe
- Take action to increase preparedness
- Improve their ability to recover from a disaster

FEMA states, "Prepareathon events mobilize people to take an active role in protecting themselves, their loved ones, and their communities." The training events cover test communication plans, drill or practice emergency response, access alerts and warnings, and document/insure your property. More than 147 million people have been through their preparation events since 2013.

Being prepared isn't tilting at windmills! Protecting your family is a serious endeavor; you are not alone in this effort. One last tip before you go is to keep your car's fuel at half full or above. I know most of us wait until we really need gas before we fill up. In an emergency, gas can be one of the first items to go. Make sure you can always drive at least a hundred miles or more before you would need to stop.

Best of luck in your endeavors, and use the resources listed at the end of the book to help your preparedness!

Resources:

The following list is provided to you as sources of information on preparedness. You should be reviewing these sites long before you need them. There is significant data and other links from these sites to link you with other agencies, even state and local sites, in some cases. Don't wait for an emergency; websites and communication could already be lost; check these sites out as part of your planning!

Federal Agency	Website
Federal Emergency Management (FEMA)	http://www.fema.gov
Environmental Protection Agency (EPA), Chemical Emergency Preparedness and Prevention Office (CEPPO)	http://www.epa.gov/ceppo
National Domestic Preparedness Consortium	http://www.ndpc.us
National Domestic Preparedness Office (NDPO)	http://www.fas.org/irp/agency/doj/fbi/ndpo/
Department of Justice, Office for Domestic Preparedness	http://www.doi.gov

Federal Agency	Website
Nuclear Regulatory Commission (NRC)	http://www.nrc.gov
Office of Homeland Security	http://www.whitehouse.gov/homeland
U.S. National Response Team (NRT)	http://www.nrt.org
Department of Transportation (DOT)	http://www.dot.gov
American Red Cross	http://www.redcross.org
Central Intelligence Agency (CIA)	http://www.cia.gov
Department of Agriculture (USDA)	http://www.usda.gov
Department of Defense (DoD)	http://www.dod.gov
Department of Energy (DOE)	http://www.energy.gov
Dept. of Health and Human Services (HHS)	http://www.hhs.gov
HHS National Disaster Medical System (NDMS)	http://ndms.dhhs.gov/NDMS/ndms.html
Department of Interior (DOI)	http://www.doi.gov

Federal Agency	Website
Federal Bureau of Investigation (FBI)	http://www.fbi.gov
Transportation Security Administration (TSA)	http://www.tsa.gov
Department of Transportation (DOT)	http://www.dot.gov
Department of State	http://www.state.gov
Department of the Treasury	http://www.treasury.gov

Besides all the government resources, numerous apps can help you. I have no interest in the promotion or use of these phone applications. I show them to let you know the types of apps you can find and use to be prepared.

Our Emergency Plans

Alerts & family response plans

GET

In-App Purchases

4.4 Stars

Applications like this let you put together your emergency plan and send personal alerts to others you have added to your group.

The FEMA resource is beneficial in identifying the steps you need to take. Items mentioned in this book and tips on mitigating risks align with FEMA information. You can subscribe to receive continuing tips.

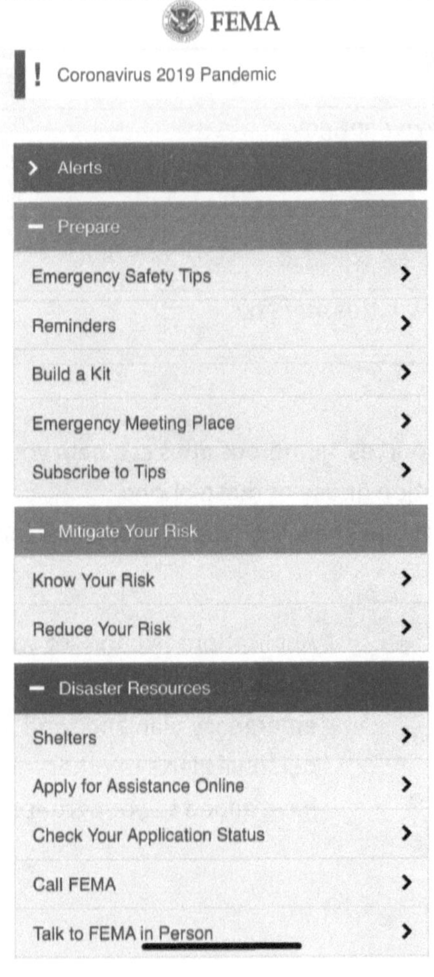

If you are involved in a declared Federal Emergency, this is the agency that helps you address the disaster and provide support. Use this site for both before and after support.

www.ingramcontent.com/pod-product-compliance
Lightning Source LLC
Chambersburg PA
CBHW031123250726
48655CB00004B/1818